BROKEN BOUNDARIES
Broken Lives

Joy P. Gage

ACCENT BOOKS

Denver, Colorado

ACCENT BOOKS
A division of Accent Publications, Inc.
12100 W. Sixth Avenue
P.O. Box 15337
Denver, Colorado 80215

Copyright © 1981 Accent Publications, Inc.
Printed in the United States of America

Library of Congress Catalog Card Number: 81-66134

ISBN 0-89636-068-7

for boundaries
which guided my life
and for music
which filled my days
I am forever grateful
to B.F.P.,
my father

This is a book for parents . . .

or maybe even grandparents. And all assorted individuals who work with other people's kids.

Part of this book is for youth. Specifically for those who face conflict with authority. Or who look at life in desperation wishing they could start over again.

It is a book about parental boundaries. Why are they set? How are they broken? And what does it matter anyway? Then there are some knotty problems. And complicated issues. Such as how can we protect the children and yet not destroy the family.

It is a book that asks a lot of questions.

Hopefully its readers will find answers.

CONTENTS

In Search of Rights

1

In Search of Rights

Should schools be integrated? Should women have equal rights with men? Should children have the right to develop their own values? Should homosexuals be recognized as a minority group? The questions, issues, groups and voices continue to multiply as the search for human rights gains momentum.

As fresh issues arise, advocate groups are formed and new voices are heard. The result is often seen as a frenzied race for unconditional freedom. But there seems to be a general reluctance among the equal rights advocates to deal with the inevitable question, "What happens when your rights interfere with mine?"

Ignoring mounting legal confusion, those fighting for rights continue to move toward a society which would impose no boundaries upon its citizens.

Balancing rights in the past

The issue of human rights has long been a catalyst for common causes. Throughout history people have joined in mass demonstrations whereby wrongs have been made right, liberty has been restored, freedom has been won, movements have been spawned.

In defense of their rights, men have carried arms, done battle, laid down their lives. Families have fled homelands, risked precarious ocean voyages, established new frontiers. Kings have been defied, governments formed, laws enacted.

Preservation of rights has necessarily involved both the protection of society as a whole and the protection of the rights of the individual citizen. Historically, such a balance has proved difficult to maintain. Some of history's most heinous crimes have been committed by rulers who acted in behalf of society while ignoring the rights of the individual.

Josephus, the Jewish historian, records a mothers' march on Jerusalem which culminated with a sit-in at the temple. (Students in the sixties did not invent this popular protest method.) The mothers staged the demonstration to protest the death of their sons—robbers, all—who had been executed without benefit of trial. The right of every citizen to a trial before the Sanhedrin had been ignored by the Governor of Galilee in a zealous attempt to rid the country of pesky thieves.

It was a shrewd political move. Many citizens responded by singing the Governor's praises in the streets. But the more perceptive among them recognized that the rights of the individual had been threatened. They lamented the loss of liberty, if not the loss of lives.

Their astute observation was that a man who protected society at the expense of individual rights was a man to be feared. Their fears proved to be well-founded. The Governor of Galilee rose to become their king. In history he is known as Herod the Great. In an age of barbarians, he distinguished himself as the most barbaric of all.

Modern history illustrates what can happen when a mad dictator devises a master plan in which individuals are dispensable for the good of society. The atrocities of Hitler's regime are graphically portrayed in a museum at Dachau, a former concentration camp.

We visited this memorial with two of our daughters while they were still in their teens. It was a life-changing experience for both of them. Face to face with grim reminders of the recent past, they encountered the reality of man's inhumanity to man. Like countless other visitors to Dachau they voiced the unanswerable question, "How could one human being do this to another?"

The museum at Dachau attempts to answer the question in part by illustrating the steps which led to the atrocities. The warning that the loss of liberty leads to loss of life is embodied in the quotation: "Where books are burned, bodies will also be burned." The ovens of Dachau still stand in mute testimony to a time when too few protested too little too late.

When rights swing out of balance

Our modern fight for rights has little to do with mad dictators or shrewd political endeavors. Today the pendulum has swung to the quest for individual lifestyles—looking out for "number one" by erasing archaic boundaries.

A proliferation of movements—civil rights, women's rights, youth rights, "gay" rights—attests to the fact that society is determined to create a legal Utopia where every man, woman and child has the right to pursue his own desires.

So far no one has found a way to guarantee justice for all. Amidst positive victories, these movements have also produced negative consequences. Charges of reverse discrimination, violation of separation of church and state laws, erosion of the family unit, and an almost total collapse of any parental support system are but a few casualties of a permissive society.

In 1978, a legal precedent was set when the United States Supreme Court upheld a reverse discrimination charge brought by Bakke, a white medical student at the University of California at Davis. In another case, which clearly tested separation of church and state laws, a San Francisco church was sued by the Gay Rights Organization for firing a homosexual organist.

In Arizona, a school board was forced to tangle with the question, "Will we infringe on the right of the child if we inform parents of the sexual activities of eight- and nine-year-old girls?"

As the quest for individual rights continues, it becomes progressively personal and increasingly bizarre. A California high school student was dismissed from school for wearing an obscene button to class. With the aid of

14

the American Civil Liberties Union, he sued the school for infringing on his personal rights.

Across the continent another young boy won his fight for personal freedom when a judge declared that the student must be permitted to take his homosexual boyfriend to the high school prom.

Not surprisingly, schools and city governments are hesitant to take action concerning offensive activities for fear of being charged with violating someone's constitutional rights.

News commentators tell us that never in our nation's history has there been a generation which has been so liberated, so endowed with rights, so unrestricted, so free to live and let live. Yet, listening to a sobbing fifteen-year-old girl verbalize the guilt she felt over an abortion, I sensed that she had found little comfort in her liberation or her legal rights. In spite of such reasoning as, "It's your right," "It's your life," "It's your body," "It's your choice," she had discovered too late that her conscience could not live with her decision.

As I looked into that twisted, tormented face I thought of those who would inform this girl of her rights. There are welfare dollars to help support her chosen lifestyle. There are statisticians to keep the public informed on that lifestyle. But after the free clinics, the social agents and the statisticians have done their work, who will help her pick up the pieces of her broken life and begin again?

Who will tally the violated consciences of children, barely in their teens, who are already saying, "I wish I had my life to live over again"? How can we measure human cost? What can we say to a benevolent society which has yet to learn that where boundaries are broken, lives will be broken?

The
Purpose of
Parental
Boundaries

2

The Purpose of Parental Boundaries

Parental boundaries are viewed differently by various people. The adolescent in conflict with his parents over restrictions sees parental boundaries as something to be escaped. In his eyes the arbitrary standards which determine such boundaries are designed to make life as miserable as possible. "Who needs boundaries?" he asks.

Certain elements of society see parental boundaries as part of a plot by parents to impose their lifestyle on their kids. "Kids are not parental property," they reason. "They have their own rights."

Relatively few people see that, in reality, the primary purpose of parental boundaries is one of protection. Telling a child "no" until he is old enough to make wiser decisions does more than impose the parents' standard. It protects the child from making decisions from too small a perspective. It protects him from making decisions which will alter his life for years to come. It protects the child until he is legally old enough to accept the responsibilities of his decisions.

The erosion of parental rights

Parents are finding it increasingly difficult to protect their minor children; the parental right to set boundaries for the child is being eroded on every hand. Erosion of the parents' right and responsibility to set boundaries is inadvertently and aggressively being accomplished through legislation, through social agents, through schools. While some parental limits are being legally removed, others simply disappear because parents no longer care enough to spend the time required to maintain them.

We live in selfish times. The mother whose chief aim is to seek her own identity may soon find that the teenage daughter gets in her way. And the teenager who believes that, by virtue of his existence, he is entitled to all the privileges of the adult world may find that his parents cramp his lifestyle.

Meanwhile, on every hand experts on adolescents convey the message, "We understand teens are doing everything there is to do anyway. Our job is to help them do it responsibly." No thought whatever seems to be given to the effect such permissive irresponsibility will have on parents or the total family unit.

The elusive goal

As a high school student, I participated in a number of oratorical contests in which I was required to research, write and memorize a speech on some aspect of the United States Constitution. In the research process I learned an important concept regarding rights: There is no such thing as *unlimited* individual freedom. Freedom demands choices. Choosing one freedom often necessitates the limitation of another. A democracy has within it the seeds of its own destruction; therefore, a certain responsibility is demanded of those who would preserve it.

This basic concept seems to have become largely obscured by society's current obsession with the right of the individual. More than 300 years ago, John Donne wrote that "no man is an island unto himself." But the American public remains unconvinced. Our quest for total freedom for the individual is an elusive goal.

Nowhere is confusion over individual rights more evident than in the conflict between parental rights and children's rights. The term, parental rights, does not appear to have a legal definition. In a day when everyone is fighting for someone's rights, the right of the parent seems to be one cause without an advocate.

The children's rights furor

In the battle over children's rights, the parent has become the first casualty. His authority has been eroded, his position usurped, his role redefined.

As early as 1976, the children's rights movement was summarized as a "low profile movement aimed beyond child abuse problems to provide distinct constitutional rights for children." At the time there were groups vigorously working for the cause in every major city in twenty-four states.

Robert A. Burt expresses his concern in his book, *Children's Rights, Contemporary Perspectives.* "In my view," writes Burt, "children cannot be adequately or even sensibly protected by giving them 'rights' that state officials will enforce against parents. Children can only be protected by giving them parents. The children's rights movement today is in danger of ignoring this simple homely truth, and thus disservicing the best interests of children."

The issue of children's rights is so emotionally explosive that it is difficult for a group to discuss it intelligently and objectively. Recently, at a national convention of an evangelical denomination, I witnessed delegates discussing a resolution dealing with forces which threaten the home, parental authority and children. While the proposed resolution passed, it was only after much heated discussion.

Those whose sad job it is to handle abused children interpreted the resolution as a lack of concern for thousands of children who every year are abused, beaten and sometimes killed in their homes. Others simply interpreted it as a statement that the delegates are acutely aware of potentially threatening intervention into the American home.

It seems to me to be quite essential to the survival of both the child and the home that we begin to make some distinction between real and imagined child abuse. Parents who are guilty of this despicable crime should be stopped. Such situations demand intervention. No child should have to remain in a home where he lives with the prospect of permanent disability or death at the hands of his parents. But such intervention should be limited to situations where it is clear that the child needs new parents and where the state is prepared to find new parents who are willing to take the continuing responsibility of raising the child.

Admittedly, we need laws to protect children from physical abuse. But legislation which reaches beyond the issue of child abuse represents a serious intrusion into the home.

I began this project out of concern for the parent. "How can the parent be held responsible for a child over whom he has little legal control?" I asked. I soon realized there was a question of far greater significance: "How can a parent protect a child when the law allows that child to be so easily exploited?"

There are parents who desire more than anything to protect their children from becoming enmeshed in drugs, sex and liquor until those children become adults. At best, it may be that, with a few more years' experience, the children will make wiser decisions. At worst, they will legally be responsible for whatever actions they choose to take as adults.

Protecting the child

As a parent, I am most alarmed at signs which indicate a lack of distinction between protecting a child and protecting the *rights* of a child. Protecting rights involves helping the child to make personal choices regardless of parental opinion, often without parental knowledge or consent. Protecting rights involves fighting for legislation which guarantees the child the right to make choices, the consequences of which he may not be fully prepared to accept.

On the other hand, protecting the child involves making some choices for him, setting rules, determining curfews, screening associates and delaying certain rights until the child reaches the age of legal responsibility. It means fighting legislation which allows exploitation of the child. It means fighting for legislation to protect the *child.*

In Mill Valley, California, a group of concerned parents pleaded with their city council to put shops selling drug paraphernalia off limits to children. As reported in San Rafael's *The Independent Journal* (January, 1980), an astute statement was made by a mother who received loud applause when she told the council, "Children don't mind being exploited. They are eager to be in—they don't dwell on the consequences . . . we adults must take the responsibility where children are too naive to protect themselves."

Parents are in the business of setting protective boundaries. When those boundaries are removed a child may be exploited, even by those who express concern for his rights.

Setting aside the issue of parental rights, let us think about the question, "What is best for the child?" Are we helping young people become responsible by giving them rights which allow them to step outside parental boundaries prematurely? On every hand, young people are being intellectually convinced that they have the right to develop their own lifestyle according to socially accepted norms which may have little to do with parental values. These lifestyles have produced statistics which now include one million teenage pregnancies a year, over half conceived out of wedlock. In terms of welfare dollars, the statistics show five billion per annum.

There are statistics to show how many babies are unwanted, how many are kept, how many are aborted. There are statistics on venereal disease and cervical cancer. There are even statistics to show the special health hazards of children having children and that family planning has not affected those statistics one bit. But as yet no statistics have been compiled on what happens when young people learn too late that some rights can be very wrong and that an intellectual knowledge of accepted norms cannot quiet the conscience.

This book is an attempt to show that broken boundaries result in broken lives and specific forces are constantly working to erode those boundaries. But there are practical ways to counterattack the forces and, when lives *are* broken, it is not the end. Broken lives can be rebuilt.

Development and Value of Parental Boundaries

3

Development and Value of Parental Boundaries

Life is full of boundaries. Your front door constitutes a boundary to the rest of the world. On the job, boundaries are formed by areas restricted for designated personnel. Recreation areas have boundaries to separate the swimmers from the boaters. Daily, we grow accustomed to boundaries, realizing that they are necessary for the protection of property and lives.

Geographical boundaries in the home

From the very beginning, parents are in the business of

setting protective boundaries. One of the first things a parent does for his child is to establish geographical boundaries. The infant is brought home from the hospital and placed within a bassinet or a crib because this is safer than a bed or a couch with no railings.

The playpen provides a safe place for the child who has learned to sit up. Folding gates installed at stairways become protective boundaries for the toddler at play. The fenced back yard often constitutes a geographical boundary for the preschooler.

No one questions the theory that such restrictions are necessary for the protection of the child. At no time is the toddler allowed to play in the street. In fact, a dash into the street after a ball is apt to be rewarded with a spanking to remind him the street is off limits. This is such a fundamental rule that even strangers know when a child has slipped through accepted boundaries.

Once while driving through the City of Sacramento, my husband spotted a toddler standing at the corner of a busy intersection. The three of us in the car knew the child was in immediate danger. My husband quickly pulled over to the curb and parked. We were able to avert a potential tragedy by persuading the child to go home.

Although the child had shown no fear of the fast moving traffic, he was frightened when I approached him. He quickly ran halfway down the block to the front door of a house, crying all the way. Before returning to our car I made sure that the child was safe.

The danger of removing boundaries prematurely

It can be tragic if the child fails to respect parental boundaries. It is unthinkable that a parent would remove them prematurely. Where the safety of a child is concerned, no parent is going to accept defeat lightly.

Imagine a mother shrugging her shoulders and saying, "I can't keep that child out of the street, so I tell him, 'If you must play in the street, do it in front of your own house.'"

Boundaries are changed as the child grows, but always with the safety of the child in mind. Some boundaries will be removed after the child is taught responsibility. The child entering kindergarten is no longer told, "Don't go into the street." Instead, he is taken to the corner and told, "Look in each direction for cars, cross only when it is safe and only here at the corner."

Reinforcement of parental boundaries

The kindergarten teacher often reinforces what the parents teach by giving safety instruction. I always appreciated this because in our experience the kindergarten teacher was quickly accepted as an authority figure. Whatever she said made an indelible impression on the little one experiencing life outside the home for the first time.

Two of our daughters attended kindergarten under the same teacher. As part of the daily routine, Mrs. Lee always lined the children up at the classroom door at dismissal time. While standing in line they sang a song about watching out for cars and never riding with strangers. It was the last thing they did each day and it made a great impression on our daughters, especially our youngest.

One day she arrived at school and decided that she had come too early. Now, there were strict rules about coming too early so she promptly turned around and ran home. In the meantime I had gone to my husband's office so there was no one home and the door was locked.

31

When Mrs. Lee missed our daughter she asked a few questions and determined that some investigation was warranted. The principal's wife was in the building and volunteered to go looking for the missing pupil. She found our daughter sitting rather forlornly on the front steps of our home. But when she offered to take our daughter back to school, she refused to go. She knew the principal, but this woman was a stranger and Mrs. Lee had taught them not to get into a car with a stranger.

She would have taken the stranger into the house to make a telephone call if they could have gotten in! (There was nothing in the song about that danger—or else they left out a verse, I guess!) The problem was finally resolved when they went across the street to a neighbor whom they both knew and there contacted us by telephone.

For the most part, I believe that children grow up accepting boundaries as a necessary part of life. If on occasion they overstep them, there is usually a cut, a bruise, a fall, or a close call to remind them that parental boundaries are for their own good.

Transition from geographical to moral boundaries

Long after the bassinets, the playpens, the folding gates and the fenced yards are forgotten, the parent still has boundaries which he believes are essential for the protection of the child. But physical boundaries are gradually replaced with moral boundaries and it becomes harder for the child to accept parental restrictions. This is not to say that the moral training of the child begins at a much later age. It should, in fact, begin very early. But as the child grows, the more evident boundaries are of a moral nature. By the time the child is a teenager most parental boundaries fall into the moral category.

Often the single greatest problem in the teenagers' daily routine is that of conflict over parental boundaries. "Don't drink!" "Don't take drugs!" "Don't smoke!" "Don't get involved in premarital sex!" The parent knows that these admonitions carry physical as well as moral implications, but to the teenager the daily warnings begin to sound like overstated rhetoric. They seem as redundant as that sign in the San Diego Zoo which reads:

> Please do not
> annoy, torment, pester, plague,
> molest, worry, badger, harry,
> harass, heckle, persecute, irk,
> bullyrag, vex, disquiet, grate,
> beset, bother, tease, nettle,
> tantalize, or
> ruffle the animals.

At this point, conflict between parent and child begins to grow. The teenager seeks independence of parental boundaries. The parent overemphasizes whatever he feels Johnny isn't hearing.

Support of parental boundaries disappears

Experience as a parent has never been a criterion for giving unsolicited advice on the subject. Counselors, teachers, relatives and assorted acquaintances offer advice on what the parent should or should not do. For years parental restrictions have been analyzed and criticized by well-meaning outsiders. There is no other job in society which comes under so much scrutiny by the inexperienced, the ill-informed and the ill-advised. This is especially true in respect to parenting teenagers. When the child reaches the teen years, suddenly it becomes everyone's prerogative to preempt the parent.

Any support system the parent may have previously felt seems to have disappeared. Physical boundaries are easily understood. Moral boundaries are more complex. Total strangers may rescue children from physical danger. Kindergarten teachers may reinforce parental safety training but no one seems to see the need to support parental restrictions of a moral nature on the teenager. In fact, the very right to set those restrictions is receiving increasingly less public support.

Parental right to impose boundaries questioned

In the past the *wisdom* of parental restrictions was sometimes questioned. Everyone except the parent in question seemed to know whether those restrictions were too lenient or too confining. But no one presumed to question the parents' *right* to set restrictions. In other words, people may have doubted parental *ability* to control a child, but no one doubted his *right* to try. Not so today. Now it is the parental right to control the child which is under scrutiny.

The disappearing economic control factor

Formerly, one of the chief control factors in teenage rebellion was that of economics. A minor would not easily throw over parental restrictions because he depended upon his parents for support. Responsibility for oneself was seen to be the price of freedom.

This concept, I believe, was recognized by both parent and child. The parent, while not necessarily agreeing with the minor's actions, recognized that financial independence earned the minor the right to ignore parental restrictions. The minor recognized that without such independence he would have to respect the restrictions of those who supported him. It was the old concept that responsibility accompanies rights.

Unfortunately this is changing. Official and unofficial help is readily available to minors who opt for freedom from parental boundaries. Today's teenager has at his disposal an amazing array of people who provide every conceivable type of service. Whether the need is for shelter, food, or legal aid, there is someone readily available to help the minor child. In some communities agencies provide traveling legal aid from a van and pass out business cards to the teen population. The services are free. Thus, the economic control factor is becoming a thing of the past.

People who work with other people's kids

There are professional volunteers as well as non-professionals who take an interest in teens. Many of them talk like, dress like, and act like teenagers. Their chief message is apt to be, "We understand you," which is great if it does not translate, "We know your parents *don't* understand you."

I would be the first to admit that in many cases a third party may be more objective than parents. But what they have in objectivity must be balanced with what they lack in facts. It is easy to offer friendship and understanding to one with whom your life is not involved. With limited knowledge of Johnny or Johnny's family, it is easy to make assumptions which do not represent the total picture. The parent who lives with the child, who sees him in every type of mood, and has nourished and cared for him since birth, sees a completely different picture.

Susan left home and went to live with a family in her community who offered an open door to all teens of the community who were in conflict with their parents. Susan chose to live with them because she did not like the responsibilities laid upon her at home. After two weeks the family threw her out because they saw a different side of her. She was an irresponsible girl and her lack of responsibility got on their nerves.

There may be little that a parent can do to prevent Johnny or Susie from leaving home today. The wise parent must seize whatever opportunity presents itself to impress upon the child the implications of the decision to leave home.

Larry was just sixteen when he decided he did not need parental restrictions complicating his life. He rather quickly found a couple who would take him in. After ten days or so, the couple called Larry's parents and suggested that, inasmuch as they were now caring for Larry's needs, the parents might wish to contribute some support money. Larry's mother responded by saying, "As long as Larry is at home, we take care of all his needs. But if you are assuming responsibility for him, you must take care of those needs." The parents refused to support Larry as long as he was not under their roof. It does not surprise me that Larry now has excellent rapport with his parents and that he learned to respect them and their philosophy.

People who get involved in teenagers' lives should be careful about giving options to parental restrictions. The period of conflict is such a short period of life for the young person. How can an outsider judge what a child may learn by working through a difficult situation with his parents?

Limited objectivity of parents

Parents are often criticized for their lack of objectivity. It is true that as parents we must strive to be objective in our decisions. Restrictions should not be imposed out of reaction to what an older brother did or as a result of some exaggerated fear. But to strive for total objectivity in the parent-child relationship is unrealistic. A parent would have to be very cold and calculating to act with total objectivity.

What kind of parent would any of us be if we were able to treat our children with the same detachment we would treat the children of a stranger, or even a neighbor? And why should anyone expect parents to demonstrate objectivity to this extent?

One of our neighbors from many years ago was an outstanding surgeon whose skills we always admired. Our children were the same age and were constant companions. He operated on our little girl. But he would not operate on his own son. He said to my husband one day, "It doesn't bother me to wade in blood so long as it belongs to someone else. But let someone in my family have a nosebleed and that is a different story." Medicine, after all, is a much more scientific field than parenting. Yet the medical profession has long recognized the inherent danger of treating one's own family.

I am afraid that total objectivity in a parent would take the heart out of parenting, reduce the position to that of a robot, and produce what we often refer to as a person without any glands.

A son accused his mother of letting her fears cloud her objectivity and ruin his good times. He thought that she hovered over him because she worried too much. The mother admitted that she was a worrier. She also told her son that mothers have always worried and that she was not of the pioneer sort so he should not expect her to change the trend.

Teenagers also lack objectivity

The teenager has his own problems with objectivity. When a teen hears advice from parents he often reacts with such classic statements as, "You are just punishing me for what my sister did," or, "Just because my brother went to college, that doesn't mean I have to go."

In fact, the teen can apply conflicting reasoning and never be aware of it. One moment Johnny says, "Why do you expect me to do everything my older brother did?" and in the next breath he says, "You let my older brother do that, why can't I?"

Sometimes the influence of a third party does help. It's possible that Johnny can listen to an adult friend without reacting. Somehow he is able to sift through all the facts without the trappings of what he considers to be parental lack of reason. Thus, there are times when the teenager will accept advice from an adult outsider which "suspiciously" resembles the parental advice he has already rejected.

In his more congenial moments the teenager regards parental boundaries as the work of overprotective parents. In his worst moments he interprets them as a lack of trust. At no time will it be easy to accept restrictions unless he is convinced they are for his own good. It is much easier to accept restrictions when the motivation is that of self-preservation or self-protection.

Once I encountered a boundary sign posted by a landowner who had obviously had some problems convincing tourists that his land was private. It was along a little back road in the Missouri Ozarks where much of the land was posted. One farmer had gone all out to state his case. "Private Property. Do not enter. No Hunting. No Trespassing. Violators will be shot. This means you."

The fact that I regarded some unseen farmer as a bit eccentric and very cantankerous did not cloud my reasoning. Assuming that my life would be in danger if I went any further, I got back into the car and rode on.

Potential problems caused by the third party

However unreasonable a minor may see parental restrictions to be, I believe that he should be encouraged to honor those restrictions. Adults who work with other people's kids should be particularly careful in this area.

Parents can accept the fact that teens need other adults in their lives. But in a crisis situation the part of the outsider becomes crucial. In too many cases when Johnny opts for breaking through parental boundaries, he is aided by a third party.

I believe that most young people benefit from the friendship of adults. A teenager needs an adult figure in his life other than his parents. Such friendships are most beneficial, however, when respect for parental authority is present. Teachers, counselors, ministers, neighbors, uncles and aunts all have the potential for becoming special persons to teens.

I am glad for such people who have filled this role in the lives of our daughters. I like to think that I fill such a role in the lives of a few young people of our acquaintance. But in order to have a positive influence on the life of the young person, these relationships must be controlled. The wise adult will be able to establish rapport with a young person without undermining the parents, and parental authority must not be threatened.

There is an old Indian proverb which says, "Never criticize a man until you have walked a mile in his moccasins." Perhaps it is time to suggest an updated version:

"Never criticize a parent until you have carried his papoose many miles upon your back."

The Changing Role of the Public School

4

The Changing Role
of the Public School

Few would argue with the idea that the American
school has somehow fallen lot to curing the ills of society.
Where once the curriculum consisted of reading, writing,
and arithmetic, now it covers everything from cults to
contraceptives.

How the revised set of responsibilities evolved may be
disputable, but of one thing we may be quite certain. As
long as the schools assume such responsibilities, or as
long as the schools are charged with such responsibilities,
there will be continual conflict with the home.

In many areas the public school represents one of the most serious threats to established parental boundaries. In protest of questionable school practices and/or curriculum, parents are removing children from the classroom in increasing numbers. Some parents teach their children at home; others send them to private schools. Some parents even go to jail over the issue of what Johnny is learning at school.

The responsibilities thrust upon the school are sometimes seen as justifiable and sometimes seen as an unwanted intrusion into the home. Parents inconsistently criticize schools for failing to spend enough time on basic education requirements, while at the same time demanding time-consuming extra programs. Programs are subjectively judged by parents on whether or not they are personally beneficial to their family rather than whether or not they fall within the realm of education.

Social change through schools

It takes very little reflection upon the subject to conclude that the use of schools as agents for social change is unwise, undesirable and unworkable. It is unwise to saddle the school with any responsibility which detracts from education. Furthermore, even if change is desired, no two families will agree on what should be changed, let alone how it should be done. For example, the problem of sexually active children and unwanted teenage pregnancies is a social problem. If the community views it as an educational problem to be solved with the school acting as the change agent, then the school must face the prospect of determining a moral code acceptable to the entire community. Realistically, this is impossible. Thus, the theory of using the school as a change agent is unworkable.

Those who willingly relegate responsibility for social change to the school must face this fundamental fact: the more one depends upon the school (or the church, or the government) to solve social problems, the more one relinquishes the right to determine what should be changed. It is highly undesirable to depend upon the school to act as a change agent unless you are content to allow the school to determine the standard by which you are to live.

Mutual support system disappearing

There was a time in our nation's history when the relationship between the home and the school could be described as a mutual support system. Parents tended to warn the children, "If you get a spanking at school, you will get another when you come home." Teachers encouraged pupils to respect parents. Teachers were charged with educating the pupil. Rarely did the educator have to make a decision which affected relationships within the home.

Obviously, this is no longer the case. Parents readily denounce the public schools. Administrators, in turn, point to unrealistic demands placed by society upon the school system.

A district superintendent who is a friend of long standing has watched changes within his district for over a quarter of a century. He is convinced that schools *reflect* society; they do not *lead* society.

"It gets bad a little bit at a time," he said. "Society today no longer reflects the Judeo-Christian mores which were this country's foundation."

In his article, "Why Our Public Schools Don't Work" (*Reader's Digest,* November 1979), John C. Sawhill places the blame for a sharp increase of functional illiteracy upon the prolonged effort to make the education system the principal tool for social change.

Beginning in the fifties, Sawhill notes, we demanded within our schools a harmony among races which in fact did not exist anywhere else. In the sixties we insisted that the schools restore social order, and in the seventies, attend to the wants of the individual.

Innovative teaching

Writing in the *New York Times,* Frank Armbruster declares that we are not getting our money's worth from public education. According to Armbruster, we are out to educate the whole person and with such an objective, teaching the child to read, write and do arithmetic can be very dull. Armbruster states that, in terms of cost and benefit, the fact is that the more parents have spent on schools, the less their children have learned. Scores on achievement tests reveal a decline in academic ability. His conclusion is that from historical, monetary, and home environment perspectives, that which most affects academic performance has been the degree to which schools sacrifice traditional disciplines and subjects for innovative activities.

As a mother who admittedly is not an educator, I have observed the effects of innovative activities in our own family and in the school districts as a whole. One of our daughters was asked to complete a standard evaluation on what the public school system had done for her. She told us that she had rather bluntly said that she felt cheated. She always happened to be in the class that was experimenting with something new and the experiments had not contributed positively toward her education.

Actually, this daughter started school with a positive

attitude, loved it and was doing quite well. But in the third grade the experiment of the year was to throw out the reading books and allow the children to read from any of forty storybooks available in the room. That year her reading skills failed to develop as they should have. It was a setback for her and only because she is a determined and motivated person did she overcome this handicap inflicted upon her by an innovative reading program.

Development of reading skills is often the target of innovative programs. One year I was amazed to discover that our high school had many young people who could not read. I sat on the systems advisory board the year the state determined that there would be no more high school diplomas given to students who failed to pass a sixth grade reading level test. Along with other members of the board, I visited the class of non-readers in our high school. Later we discussed the problems of these students with the teacher. According to her, the pupils had a reading level ranging from 0-4 grade.

"Let's face it," she told us, "I am trying to build their self-image as much as anything." I went home that day remembering another conversation with teachers at the elementary school just one year before.

"We never hold pupils back," they said, "because it is bad for their self-image." I had wondered at the time what happened to the child who was promoted but couldn't keep up. What did that do to his self-image?

Protesting public education

Marva Collins, a teacher of an all-black private school in Chicago, bases her teaching methods on reading skills. She does not believe in compromising with this skill.

"If you can't read, you can't do anything else," she

said. "I can't see why society finds this so difficult to understand. Just about all learning branches from that skill and almost every profession today demands exactness."

Citing one child as an example, she explained that the child had expressed the desire to be a surgeon. "That means learning that when you have to make a cut two centimeters to the right of a spot, you don't make it two and a half, look at it and guess it's going to be okay," she said.

Mrs. Collins' school is in a shabby west side neighborhood in an all-black, poverty level area of rundown multi-family apartments. Her school holds thirty children and there are four hundred on the waiting list.

This is but one example of protest over public education. Widespread parental protest against the public school system appears to be growing. Parents fight to maintain one-room schools because they have greater control over their children's education. Private schools are increasing in number. In one community of 45,000, three private schools opened in a single year. In other communities, committees and protest groups are formed in an attempt to stem the tide of objectionable concepts coming from the schools. The gulf becomes wider between home and school and, still, solutions cannot be found.

Textbook content has become the center of controversy in many school districts. In some communities creation versus evolution is an ongoing struggle. One California group worked long and hard to win the right to place a disclaimer statement concerning evolution in all textbooks. Others have gone further and succeeded in having creation taught as a viable theory alongside evolution.

The Mel Gablers of Longview, Texas have become

widely known for their concern about textbook content. Their interest was aroused through an incident which involved their high school age son. The son queried his father about the intent of the Constitution framers concerning states' rights. Gabler explained what was involved in states' rights. The son then explained that his textbook did not teach that concept.

From that incident grew a full-time job of textbook reviewing in which both Mr. and Mrs. Gabler are involved. Their work has earned them publicity, many honors and some verbal abuse. But today when the Gablers speak out on a textbook, many important people listen. More often than not, the Gablers' recommendations are accepted.

The Gablers review textbooks from kindergarten through high school. Their job demands reading line by line as many as 500 books in preparation for hearings. While they look for many things in the books, they categorize them as facts, skills and knowledge. A fact is better than a concept because concepts will change. One question they ask concerning a textbook is, "Is it confusing or nebulous?"

The Gablers claim that many of the textbooks contain material downgrading or belittling free enterprise and traditional American standards. Among those belittled are the role of motherhood, religion and prayer, and the home and family life.

Patriotism discouraged

On occasion I have heard young Christian professionals verbalize a lack of patriotism which I find disconcerting. One once asked, "What does the *S.S. Arizona* monument have to do with me?"

This is a difficult concept for one who lived through the dark days following the sinking of the *S.S. Arizona* at Pearl Harbor. To me, it is incredible that there could be graduates of our public schools who believe that what was done in Pearl Harbor has nothing to do with generations born after peace had been restored.

Sex education, a continuing conflict

Without a doubt the greatest battle going on in schools today concerns sex education. It has been a long, sometimes confusing, often emotional struggle.

In recent years, a couple has decided to go to jail rather than allow their children to be subjected to sex education through their school system. A group has been responsible for killing a sex education program in state schools by their intervention at the Capitol. And Southern California parents have successfully removed from the curriculum material which they considered unsuitable for their children.

But recently the issue has again been raised because of proposed new material. At this time, however, it has been shelved because parents raised such an outcry. Some of the issues involved included the bringing of contraceptives into the classroom at grade levels 4-6 and proposed field trips for grades 7-8 to a drugstore to be taught how to buy contraceptives. "Alternate lifestyles," stories on lesbianism, all were included in either the material to be studied or the suggested reading list.

Bringing about change

I have met sufficient numbers of parents who involved themselves in bringing about change to know that it can be done. And it should be done. But to involve oneself in changing issues which directly touch the home one must be willing to do his homework well. One must be up-to-date, willing to stand up for what he believes and willing to clearly define that for which he fights.

Unfortunately, Christians are notorious for substituting zeal for knowledge. I recall that in one community in which we lived a group of believers came to our door with a petition to sign. Their purpose was to get certain books out of the school. The leader showed me the samples. Certainly they were shockers. I would never want such books on our public school shelves. The tasteless pictures as well as the text were not what I considered to be proper for the lower grades for which they were designed.

However, the petition concerning a certain book was quite vague and I wasn't sure of all the group was trying to say. I questioned them about the books. Where were they used? Which schools were involved? Where had the petitioner gotten the book? I discovered that the group leader had been stirred into action through correspondence with a friend from another state. She had also obtained a copy of the book from her friend. Since the petition concerned local schools I was particularly interested in whether or not the book was being used, or considered for use, locally. But when I questioned the well-meaning petitioners, they said, "Surely you don't approve of this book?"

Later I discovered that the book was indeed published by a company which had never been used in our state and against which there was so much public opinion that there was little danger of its ever being used. How much more effective petitioners could be if they were willing to do their homework a little better.

Educational material varies from state to state and from year to year, so there is a genuine need for unending alertness on the part of the parents to avoid the risk of being simply alarmists.

The school counselor

Columnist Bryce Anderson has openly criticized a bill to muzzle school counselors. Noting that high school counselors have an open door into the home, he cites the fact that they query students on the most private matters of family life yet insist upon the right to withhold information from parents.

On the other hand, counselors are quick to point out to parents that they will withhold no information from students. Parents do not enjoy the privilege of conversing confidentially with the counselor.

In one high school, parents of an incoming freshman requested that the counselor assign their son to classes away from gang members.

The counselor responded by telling the parents, "You can't pick your child's friends for him. And in any case I would not do this without telling your son."

Our own contacts with high school counselors were always positive experiences. I believe that a counselor can be one of the most valuable contacts for both parent and child if the counselor has the proper attitude toward the home.

Whether it is an unsatisfactory counseling situation, a biased textbook, or an improperly taught sex education class, the parent should keep on top of what is going on in the school. If parental boundaries are to be preserved, parents can no longer sit idly by ignoring the changing role of the public school in family life.

The
Legal
Exploitation
of Children

5

The Legal Exploitation of Children

"Disagreements between children and their parents are a common occurrence and usually do not rise to the level of a legal question," states Hillary Rodham in writing on *Children's Rights: A Contemporary Perspective.* Rodham defends the idea of children's rights while rejecting the argument that legislation of such rights would give children the right to take their parents to court "if they were ordered to take out the garbage." According to Rodham, this argument was raised several years ago by opponents to the Child and Family Development Act.

I would caution readers, however, that Rodham is not entirely accurate, or perhaps he is just not up-to-date. While waiting for Junior to take them to court over household chores, parents should be aware of the legal implications of children's rights which already affect the home.

If it has been your assumption that your home is not likely to be touched by bizarre legislation concerning children's rights, read on.

One of the most graphic illustrations of the contradictory legal views we are facing concerns a school vaccination program in Yuma, Arizona. Because some parents failed to comply with state law to have school-age children vaccinated, the school district was asked to run a vaccination program. Parents were required to sign consent forms for the children to have the vaccination.

Confusion set in when a memo from the State Department of Health Services arrived. According to the memo, any female student approaching menarche could sign an exemption form from rubella vaccine, even though parents of said student had previously signed a consent form. This exemption was allowed because of possible birth defects which could be caused by the vaccine if the girl was pregnant or became pregnant within three months.

Discussion of the program was reported in the *Yuma Daily Sun.* According to the *Sun,* the school board president objected to the provision. She declared that deciding whether or not to take the vaccine was too much responsibility to place on a child. The director of the County Health Department countered with a statement that anyone who could become pregnant had to be counseled about the possible risk to unborn children. He noted that the mandatory provision for the vaccine was a result of initial parental neglect in not first having the children vaccinated.

Board members objected to the school nurse having to ask eight- and nine-year-olds if they were sexually active.

At issue was the question of notifying parents who had consented to the vaccination but whose consent might be overridden by the child. "Does the parent have the right to know? Are the child's rights being violated if the school informs the parent?"

As a parent already concerned about parental rights, I found the incident alarming. The idea that all mature eight- and nine-year-olds were to be confronted with the thought, "If you become pregnant within three months after you are vaccinated, your baby will likely be deformed," was sobering.

Are we now to assume that the onset of menarche categorizes every child as being sexually active? Can we possibly believe that the maturing body is automatically accompanied by a complete understanding of biology? Or does this equip the child to handle decisions of this magnitude?

I think it was at this point that I first began to ask, "Where is our search for rights leading us as a nation, and what price must we pay?"

It has been a few years since I've had a nine-year-old daughter. But still I have to venture an opinion on the basis of past experience. To be singled out by the school nurse and cautioned about the dangers of mixing rubella vaccine and sexual activity is simply too much for many nine-year-olds to handle.

While the legalities of parental rights versus children's rights were examined in the Yuma case, no one discussed the psychological and moral implications of the situation. Yet I think it reasonable to assume they exist. The occasion of the vaccine program was only one example of children being exposed to adult authorities communicating a "non-judgmental" message. The school was required in this case to communicate to the children, "We understand you have rights, including the right to be sexually active. We must apprise you of certain facts because we assume that you are sexually active." What happens when adult authority figures in the child's world continually communicate this message?

What happens to society when other non-judgmental messages are constantly communicated? On a recent news telecast on teenage pregnancy, the narrator frequently began his statements, "IF the girl decides to carry her baby full term. . . ." Whatever his intent, this man was communicating that there is an option to carrying the baby full term.

I do not know how the experts would evaluate this type of communication, but my mother instinct tells me that this is not healthy—morally or psychologically.

Age-of-consent laws

There are some very real dangers in current movements which propose certain rights for children. Of particular concern is the lowering of the age of sexual consent. This type of legislation potentially minimizes such offenses as child pornography, statutory rape, child molestation and incest.

The age of sexual consent varies from state to state. Many states are in the process of revising their laws. According to a newspaper article dated April, 1979, New Jersey has been the scene of parental outcries over a lowered age-of-consent law. The revised state penal code allows thirteen-year-olds to consent to sexual activity providing the partner is not a relative, a guardian or a supervisor (teacher, etc.), and is less than four years older.

One has to wonder about problems with implementing these laws. Do those who dispense contraceptives ask, "Is your partner more than four years older?" "Who are you sleeping with? A teacher? A relative?" Does the clinic report minors suspected of sleeping with the "wrong" person?

Statutory rape laws

Incensed over the revised penal code, New Jersey parents launched a statewide campaign to amend the code and retain age sixteen as the minimum sexual consent age. One man, a police lieutenant and father of three, stated that in his opinion children under age sixteen are not psychologically mature enough to make a decision regarding sexual activity.

Michigan was the first state to institute reform of rape statutes involving minors. But since then there has been a trend against defining rape strictly on the basis of age. Such factors as circumstances of the injury and the age of the person committing the rape are now taken into consideration also.

Maryland defines rape as a sexual offense between a person less than fourteen and a person who is under eleven years of age.

Florence Rush, who has authored a book on sexual abuse of children, was quoted in the *San Francisco Sunday Examiner and Chronicle* (May, 1980), as saying, "Sex with children has always existed. Now there is a move to legitimize it." In the article, written by Sheryl Connelly, dealing with eroticization of children, Rush alleges that the sexual revolution has expanded to include children. Author Connelly takes a hard look at exploitation of young children in movies, television and advertisements.

Removing the incest taboo

Connelly also introduces some sobering thoughts on the subject of incest. "Incest is no longer a dirty word in certain psychiatric circles," she declares. There are those who debate that the time has come to break down the final moral taboo, that of engaging children in sex. She concludes the article with a statement which echoes concern about the potential psychological damage to children engaged in sex. How will such early relationships affect future capacity for healthy sex relationships? Will children be able to relate to others without using their exploitive side?

Time magazine (April 14, 1980) tackled the question of incest. An article, "Attacking the Last Taboo," called attention to several sex researchers and noted a move to make incest an acceptable, sometimes beneficial, child-adult relationship.

"As in any propaganda campaign," the article states, "the words and terms used to describe incest are beginning to change." The phrase "child abuse" is distinguished from "consensual incest" involving a parent. "Abusive incest" is different from "positive incest." According to *Time,* some of the lobbying to make incest more acceptable springs from the fringes of the children's rights movement which insist that children be granted all the rights of adults. Some people interpret this as the right of a child to be sexually active with any partner.

Exploitation through law

One highly qualified social worker whom I interviewed expressed concern over liberalized consent laws. In her opinion it opens doors for exploitation of children in three areas: by homosexuals, by child pornographers, and through incestual relationships.

While some implications of changing consent laws are yet to be seen, one thing is quite clear: The parent has limited legal recourse to protect a minor child from sexual exploitation. In fact, parents have little encouragement from society to control the minor child's sexual activity.

Dr. Robert Wallace writes a teen column for Copley News Service, "Tween 12 and 20." He was asked by a fifteen-year-old girl how to cope with parents who disapproved of her seeing a twenty-three-year-old man.

Wallace told her that fifteen-year-old girls and twenty-three-year-old guys are taboo and added that she should make friends her own age.

There was a time when mothers of young girls could discourage the attention of older men by reminding them of the legal implications. But parents today who wish to discourage such relationships will find little support from the law.

It is time for concerned citizens to examine more closely legislation, proposed legislation, and movements which purport to be beneficial to children. It's time to look below the surface and ask who will benefit.

Who, after all, benefits from the lowered age-of-consent laws? Does anyone believe for a minute that children engaging in sex are even aware of such laws? They can only be seen as an effective means of protecting those who are of legal age against possible recrimination for engaging in sex with minors.

Children in need of protection

The need to protect children from exploitation has been acknowledged from ancient times. The code of Hammurabi in 2250 B.C. made selling something to a child or buying something from a child without power of attorney a crime punishable by death.

Today children are sold everything from candy-coated cereals to drugs to sex. Whether through the media, the campus drug dealer, or through the older sex partner, children are being exploited.

Those who care about children must determine to keep a proper perspective regarding laws enacted to protect a child's rights. Discernment must be exercised. Proposed legislation must be analyzed carefully. Above all, one thought must be kept in mind. There is no justification for any law which protects the rights of the child while failing to protect the child.

The Legal
Limbo of
Liberated
Youth

6

The Legal Limbo
of Liberated Youth

There seems to me to be something terribly obscene about a system which judges a child to be politically and legally responsible at age eighteen and morally responsible at age twelve or younger. Years before your daughter can vote or drive a car she can legally make moral decisions which may permanently alter her future.

To drink or not to drink is a decision she must forego until 18 to 21 (depending on the state in which she lives) if she does it legally. Only with your endorsement can she drive a car or enter into a contract before her eighteenth birthday. Furthermore, until she has reached that magic age, she cannot attend certain movies even if you accompany her.

However, at the tender age of twelve or younger your daughter has the personal prerogative of sleeping with whomever she chooses, regardless of your opinion on the subject. Such right is acknowledged by the law which permits her to obtain birth control devices without parental knowledge or consent. It is worth noting that six years before society sanctions her attendance at movies made for mature audiences, it pronounces her mature enough to decide for herself whether or not she will take a chance with venereal disease, unwanted pregnancies and an increased risk of cervical cancer.

Dr. C. Everett Koop, one of the world's leading pediatric surgeons, co-authored a hard-hitting article on abortion in the May, 1980 issue of *Moody Monthly*. Inconsistencies of our legal system may be illustrated in their observation that, technically, a fifteen-year-old cannot have her ears pierced without parental consent but she may have an abortion without parental knowledge. For a prick in the ear she is considered a minor in need of parental guidance. But for a procedure which carries far greater physical, emotional and psychological risks she is considered a person with rights of her own and without need of parental guidance.

Rights versus responsibility

Within my own memory there was a time when an adult was an adult, a minor was a minor, and there was very little confusion about the legal status of either. Adulthood was reached at the precise hour of midnight the day before one's twenty-first birthday. It was assumed that adults had authority over and responsibility for minors. No one talked much about the rights of either group. But such discussions as there were usually centered around the relationship between rights and responsibility.

The over-forty generation will remember the outcry of young men who were required to march off to war before they were old enough to vote. They campaigned for a lowered voting age touting their slogan, "If we're old enough to fight, we're old enough to vote." Not until 1971, however, was the voting age lowered to 18. At the heart of the campaign to change the voting age was the argument that rights accompany responsibility.

Current legislation concerning rights of minors has little concern with the issue of responsibility. Today minors have rights once reserved for adulthood, yet under the law they can neither function as, nor be held accountable as, adults. Unless the trend is reversed we can expect to see more and more confusion in the laws of the land.

Problems with implementation

Increasing legal confusion may be due in part to the fact that we simply have too many laws. Thomas Erlich, former Dean of Stanford Law School, expressed his concern over this fact in the *New York Times* magazine. To underscore his point, Erlich states that during a fourteen-year period in which the population increased by 17 percent, the number of federal court cases increased about 60 percent. More than 26,000 bills were introduced during one congress and more than 200 major federal agencies, bureaus and commissions have been created in the last fifteen years, while only a few have been abolished.

Erlich convincingly shows that sometimes there ought

not to be a law, and that a statute or regulation is not necessarily the solution to all our needs. "We rely too heavily on law as an instrument of social change," he says. According to Erlich, one of the major problems of the law is that too many laws are passed without enough concern for the problems involved in implementing the laws.

Certainly the unprecedented emphasis in recent years on the issue of individual rights has carried with it a plethora of problems in the implementation department. Common sense alone tells us that the right of one individual carried to the extreme is going to infringe upon the right of another individual. No amount of legislation can create a society in which individuals may do what they please when they please without affecting the rights of other individuals.

I carry in my notebook a newspaper cartoon of a baboon scratching his head. The accompanying caption reads, "Being a baboon means never having to say you're sorry." The implication of course is that we humans exist in a society where the rights and feelings of others must be considered.

Children's rights versus parental responsibilities

The implementation of laws regarding individual rights creates special problems for the family where rights of the child often conflict with rights and/or responsibilities of the parent.

One of the greatest areas of legal confusion for the family is found in those laws which affect runaways. These laws vary from state to state. Parents of runaway children should be aware of parental responsibilities and children's rights as defined by law in the state of residence.

In some states you will be in violation of the law for not reporting a runaway minor. In other states if you give up trying to force a minor to come home the courts may construe this as abandonment. In many cases parents are liable for medical bills, accidents and other expenses incurred by the runaway minor.

Emancipation is one approach to solving these complex problems. Simply stated, it is a legal step whereby a minor is declared responsible for himself. In some cases it may give him the right to buy insurance, get a driver's license and enter into contracts. In other cases it may do little more than free parents of financial responsibility for a child they can no longer control.

Not all states have emancipation laws. Not all social workers think there should be such laws. One social worker, in stating that there was no such law in her state, commented that she was adamantly opposed to it. "The parent should always be responsible," she said. "We never remove responsibility of the parent."

"Even when you remove their authority?" probed one mother. To that question the social worker murmured some idealistic statement about shared responsibility.

I cannot say that I believe in emancipation laws any more than did that particular social worker. But we arrive at our conclusions differently. My disagreement with the concept arrives out of a penchant for realistic solutions. In my opinion, emancipation is a non-viable concept.

*Encouraging premature independence
is counterproductive*

Recently California attempted to update its emancipation law to deal with some of the realities of runaways.

69

Under the new law, a teenager may be emancipated as young as fourteen. The parents need not approve but they must know of the emancipation. While the child is supposed to be able to support himself, part of that support can be provided through welfare.

It is questionable what real rights are gained for the principals involved. How can we justify a law which gives a young person the right to run away at fourteen? There is no way that a law can equip a fourteen-year-old to earn a living in today's competitive society. With eight million people unemployed, it makes little sense economically to allow fourteen-year-olds to be emancipated at the expense of welfare dollars.

The entire system of encouraging independence at age fourteen is counterproductive. Whatever the law may grant in terms of individual rights, in terms of economic security the individual needs an education. There is no way that fourteen-year-olds can care for themselves. Nor can they expect to have any financial security for the future.

Laws which permit minors to leave home accomplish little except to allow children to wander the streets panhandling, exploiting and being exploited.

Father Bruce Ritter is Executive Director of Covenant House and Under Twenty-One, a child care agency in New York City that specializes in caring for runaway, homeless children. According to Ritter, who was quoted in *Evangelical Newsletter* (April 20, 1979), many people are unaware of the problems of runaways and homeless children in our society—or what can happen to those children. He further states that there are over one million juveniles who run away every year in this country. According to the New York City Police estimate, there are at least 20,000 runaways under sixteen in New York

City at any given time.

According to an NBC News Special Report, the care of homeless children is the fastest growing industry in the country. This documentary estimated that there are 3,000 public and private institutions caring for some 300,000 kids. And these are just those children who are in some type of trouble. No attempt was made to document the number of shelters or homes for runaways not in trouble with the law.

Those who push for more state-supported homes cry, "Someone has to take care of these kids." Someone, yes, but should it not be, in many more cases, the parents?

There are good reasons why parents should be responsible for, and have authority over, the child until that child is legally of age. Economically, anything else is disastrous. NBC estimated that it costs between seventeen thousand and twenty-one thousand dollars per year to maintain one child in the state-supported homes. Even at the lower figure that amounts to an astronomical sum. In most cases, public funds make up fifty percent of this cost. There is no estimate of the cost in additional tax funds to care for the non-institutionalized runaways who are in shelters or programs to help the legally independent minor.

Institutional parenting

Aside from the question of economics, there is the question of institutional parenting. It has been said that a child is better off in a bad home than in a good institution. It may also be said that even good institutions have bad incidents.

Yolo County, California was the scene of an investigation of the hanging death of a seventeen-year-old boy in a group home. In a two-part report on the incident, the *Sacramento Bee* raised questions about the investigation of this death as well as a previous death in the Juvenile Hall. The article questioned the current state system of institutions and foster care. Said Davis attorney, Noreen Mazelis, concerning the case, "If there is anything that comes out of the deaths—it is that the state is no better a parent than anybody else."

The truth of this statement is further illustrated from an NBC report which disclosed some facts surrounding the closure of one Arizona-based institution. Run by a psychiatrist, the ranch for boys lost its license when an escapee from the ranch reported the use of bizarre sexual acts in the "therapy" program.

The sexually active child

Sexual activity of the minor represents another area of diminished parental authority. Just what role the parent is to play concerning the rights of the sexually active child remains an obscure legal issue. I found no one who was willing to say where the parents' rights ended and the child's rights began. But one thing is frighteningly clear. Intrusion into the home in the interest of children's rights is not limited to cases of physical or sexual abuse, starvation, or neglect of health.

From the state's viewpoint, intrusion into the home in the defense of children's rights seems also to be justified in cases of poor communication or ineffective parenting. A parent who suspects his child of being sexually active and who reacts by imposing stricter controls on that child may be regarded as unrealistic and ineffective. Such non-specific terms pose a threat to all parents who find themselves in conflict over parental responsibilities and children's rights.

To whom does the child belong?

Parents should be aware that the legal conflict with parent-child rights is not entirely the result of the issue of individual rights. In some cases the basis may be found in the state's philosophy toward the status of the child. If the state regards the child as a ward of the state, then any interpretation of rights will be affected by this philosophy.

For example, the State of Ohio does not recognize any responsibility of parent to child on the basis of the relationship. In *Law for Young People, Ohio Edition* (Newbury Press), Kevin Sheard says, "To the question, 'What do I as a parent owe my child?' Ohio has this to say: 'Strictly speaking, you don't owe him anything. But you owe it to the state to give your children care, protection and guidance.' "

There is a vast difference between being responsible for a child because he is your child and being responsible for him because you owe it to the state. In the latter, the moral obligation of parent to child is eliminated. The assumption that you as a parent have the child's best interest at heart because the child belongs to you is also conspicuously lacking.

In Ohio the parent may be liable for neglecting the training of the child to the extent that the child has no morals, but it is interesting to note that in the same state some parents have been severely threatened for sending their children to private Christian schools.

In one such incident three families faced the prospect of having their children placed in foster homes and returned to public schools. The most significant aspect of this particular case is that the parents were not charged with truancy, absence of the children from a state-accredited school. Instead the charge was neglect of minor children. This charge allowed removal of children from the home. The action was averted largely because of a mass demonstration of concerned citizens which took place on the Statehouse grounds.

Numerous cases could be cited in which parental handling of rebellious teens has been challenged. In some cases the reader would sympathize with the parents. In other cases, no doubt, the reader would question the wisdom of the parents involved. Whether or not one agrees with the parents is hardly the issue. The issue is that, if parents are to be responsible for the moral training of their children, they must be given more latitude in handling that training as their conscience dictates.

I think that it is time to re-examine the role of the law and the parent alike on the subject of minor children. It is time to look for alternatives to programs which involve controversy over parental responsibilities and children's rights. Who can say what trends might be reversed if the law encouraged rather than discouraged parental control? What positive changes might be brought about if the law concerned itself with abused children more and ineffective parents less?

I believe the law should support the parents' attempts to instill moral values in the child. Where laws conflict, there ought not to be a law. If parents are to be responsible for the moral training of the children we should be able to expect support from our legal system. In my opinion, that support would better come from a non-interference policy than from more laws.

Parents must be allowed to determine the moral values for the individual home. They must also be allowed to teach those values without unnecessary interference. If this responsibility is removed from the parents, who among us is prepared to accept the alternative?

The
Role of
the Social
Worker

7

The Role of
the Social Worker

"Our job is to convince the family that they should welcome our interference," said the social worker in charge of a seminar on child abuse. She came laden with facts and films, books and bibliographies. It was obvious that she believed in what she was doing. She was confident, trained and educated. She was also young. And she had no children.

She easily demonstrated that legal intervention is necessary for the survival of a child who is physically abused. She was not so convincing when she suggested that ineffective parenting also warranted intervention. The fact that she had not yet faced the realities of parenthood spoke more loudly to the room of parents and grandparents than did her impressive credentials. Weighed against that lack, her words seemed to be untried theories and idealistic solutions.

After all, who is to be the judge of effective or ineffective parenting? I looked around the room. Should this task be given to the handful of college students present? Or would their objectivity be clouded by current conflict with parents? Could the parents in the room determine their own effectiveness? Or those few grandparents present? Perhaps the minister's wife busily taking notes? Or should it be this childless social worker?

Admittedly, it was difficult for me to be objective about some of the speaker's remarks. But I had come prepared to listen. I had expected to learn about child abuse, its cause and prevention. Still, I was surprised at her candidness. She impressed upon the group the fact that the social worker employs more power than does the court. It is possible for the social worker to remove a child from a home immediately if she believes the child to be in danger. This action is reserved only for the social worker. In her own words, "The authority of a social worker is scary."

The power of decisions

One of the most frightening things about the power of the social worker is that it is vested in a person and that person must make on-the-spot decisions.

With the need for immediate decision, I have no quarrel. I was once awakened early on a warm summer morning by screams from the adjoining row of houses.

Through the windows thrust open to invite a cooling breeze, I had unintentionally invaded the privacy of another's home. The unmistakable sounds of a raging mother and a frightened child confronted me with the question, "Is a child being beaten?" Later, convinced that this was not the case, I tried to put the matter aside. But I could not forget the sound and I had to reflect on the potential tragedies which exist behind closed doors.

But I am not sure that I concur with the idea that the social worker should be the one to intervene. I am not convinced that a social agent should employ more power than the courts. The thought of it makes me nervous.

By attending the seminar I had hoped to find specific reasons, as well as limitations, for outside interference into family problems. With that in mind I raised a question concerning fifteen-year-old Rachel (not her real name).

Rachel's case had been reviewed by a legislator on a local radio station. Rachel had some serious problems in her life. One day her father was discussing the problems with her and there was a rather ugly confrontation. The girl became very angry, went to school, told the counselor that she would not return home and was put in touch with a social worker. Within twenty-four hours she had been placed in a foster care situation. She became a chronic runaway from every foster home, yet every attempt to have the girl returned to her parents failed. At the time the legislator related the case, nothing had been resolved.

My question to the social worker was, "Since there was no charge of child abuse on the part of the parents and since there was no charge against Rachel, on what grounds was she removed from her home?"

Much to my surprise, the seemingly objective social worker responded with some biting criticism of the legislator who had reported the case. Although I had not given his name, she identified him and declared that he did not approve of what the social workers were doing and that he was against the foster care program.

Noting that she had not answered the question I persisted, "But why was that girl removed from her parents?"

Although she said she was not personally familiar with the case, the social worker ventured an opinion.

"That girl was a chronic runaway the minute she walked into the counselor's office," she said. "I can just see it now. Every time she comes home late, her father will give her the third degree. He will probably ground her for thirty days or confine her to her room. I can see the iron grills coming up over the windows."

I had not caught a vision of all that myself; however I conceded that it could happen and that it certainly would constitute an extreme form of parental control. "But is it against the law?" I asked.

"It's ineffective," she declared. "It is unrealistic and such measures will not help the situation."

I went home knowing that for me the seminar had raised more questions than it had answered. It frightened me to think that in America parents may face the prospect of having their children removed from the home when their methods of discipline are judged ineffective or unrealistic.

The potential of misused power

After months of research I still have not determined to my satisfaction whether incidents such as Rachel's are isolated or whether they point to a national trend. I have spoken to numerous professionals (including some social workers whom I greatly admire) on the subject. Some say this is not a trend. Some say we must accept a certain amount of intrusion for lesser causes in order to protect abused children. None argued the fact that the potential for widespread intrusion into the home does exist.

One of the first persons to whom I talked was a reporter. A parent and a member of a statewide committee working with deprived children, this man frankly discussed the foster care system. He assured me that there were so many legitimate needs for the foster care program that there were not enough funds to support them all. While admitting that the potential exists for unwarranted removal of children from homes, he felt that the lack of funds for foster care minimizes this threat. For my part, I found little comfort from the fact that this potential intrusion is avoided chiefly because of an economic factor.

Children are placed in foster homes for a variety of reasons. Sometimes the foster home is an alternative to an orphanage, sometimes an alternative to Juvenile Hall. The foster care system has been widely criticized by legislators, news commentators and psychologists. One Phoenix radio reporter called it a good idea gone wrong. Elsewhere, claims are made that children, even adoptable ones, are pushed from one foster home to another. In most cases foster parents are not allowed to adopt children. Yet some children literally grow up in foster homes.

A San Francisco sociologist declares that, as an alternative to Juvenile Hall, the foster home is like a slap on the wrist. Children placed in foster care under these circumstances may be guilty of a felony yet still attend public school and are out on the streets with the rest of society.

A reporter whom I have known for many years directs her criticism to the welfare department and their misuse of power. It is the unwise, overused display of authority which presents the real threat to the family, as she explains it. In a series of articles on the problem within her own state she reported the following case.

Following a tragic shooting accident in a home, three children were taken from their parents by a social worker. The details of the accident were much like those of other home accidents. An older child managed to get a gun belonging to the father and accidentally shot a younger child. The children were removed from the home and each was placed in a different foster home.

The parents were given no information as to where the children were, when or if they would be returned to the home. Although there had been no problems before with neglect of the children, or abuse, these distraught parents were told that the children were removed because they were not being cared for.

The townspeople rose up in support of the parents who were well respected. After several days, when no cause was shown to remove the children, they were returned to their parents. When interviewed, the older boy who had done the shooting said he thought the people came and took him and his brothers away because he had been a bad boy.

"Can you imagine the psychological impact on those youngsters?" wrote my reporter friend. I think that I can. Many years ago there was such an accident in the home of one of my cousins. How much greater would their sorrow have been had they been subjected to this type of treatment.

Who judges effective parenting?

Determining what to do in a case of probable abuse

certainly calls for careful consideration of all the facts. Yet going beyond abuse to examine homes to determine ineffective or unrealistic parenting presents an even greater challenge. If the social worker is to remove children for reasons of emotional neglect, ineffective parenting or unrealistic parenting, someone must determine the standard by which all parenting is to be judged.

I am totally against such a practice but I determined to find out what might be considered ineffective parenting. In the public library I found an abundance of books concerning social work, abused children, neglected children, emotionally neglected children and the proposed solutions.

One book even contained a copy of an evaluation test suggested as an aid to social workers in determining when a child was emotionally neglected. Two things were immediately evident: (1) Because the worker had to do the evaluation from observation (without prying questions), it was of necessity superficial; and (2) The nature of the questions indicated that there would be a continual need for revising the test. In fact, in light of current roles for women, the test was already considerably out of date.

Nevertheless, I examined it carefully. My curiosity was aroused. How might a social worker have evaluated my own childhood on the basis of such a test? My husband's? Or our own children's? What about the children of our psychologist friend?

The results were more amusing than enlightening. No one fared very well. I, who grew up feeling quite secure, received only marginal care according to the test. I would have been judged as a rather severely neglected child. Although most of my growing up years were spent under marginal economic conditions, I was never neglected.

The fact is, a child can grow up poor and still feel very

secure. In my own case, I was aware that we had very little, yet I grew up knowing that whatever I needed would be provided somehow by my parents. I was not concerned with the problems involved because I lived in a carefree world where the adults were in charge of the problem-and-worry department. Surely that is the best gift a parent can offer a child. The time comes soon enough for the child to enter the adult world with all of its concerns.

It surprised me that, whereas parents are constantly criticized for giving children things instead of time and love, here was a standard which obviously penalized parents who could not give material things.

The standard also showed prejudice against parents who do not assume the traditional roles. Children should grow up in homes where Mother depends on Father for masculine tasks, expresses pride in daughter's femininity or son's masculinity and openly expresses the feeling that her job is the housework. In homes where the mothers do not fit the traditional role, children may be judged as having marginal child care.

I am a very traditionally-minded mother. Our family followed rather traditional lines in the roles in the home; however, in defense of mothers who do not fit this role, I have to say that the test is unfair. Within our circle of friends we have several strong examples of untraditional husband/wife roles. Children in the home are not being exposed to the same concept of mother and father as were our children. Whether or not I agree with their approach has nothing to do with the issue. The issue is, "Does the absence of strong male and female roles constitute marginal child care?" I think my friends would argue the point, and rightfully so.

I would not want to imply that this test is being routinely used. I am sure this is not the case. I mention the test only as a reminder that there are constant forces outside the family trying to determine what constitutes effective parenting.

Concerning the potential need for a uniform standard of child rearing, Sanford N. Katz in *When Parents Fail* (Beacon Press, 1971) says: "Until society reaches the point of determining the exact 'formula' for molding 'ideal' or 'normal' citizens, and unless total uniformity among our citizens is desired, there does not appear to be any clear basis for preferring one particular form of child rearing over another and permitting intervention for deviation from that mode."

With boundaries broken, what are the options?

Erosion of parental boundaries places parent and child at odds with one another. Such boundaries have long existed. At times these boundaries are narrow and confining. At times they are so broad as to appear non-existent. But they do exist. It is safe to say that parents have always been criticized for the boundaries they set. But their legal right to impose such restrictions was not challenged.

The fact that this right of parents is now being challenged raises an important question. If parents cannot restrict children, what are the options? Will children go unrestricted? Or will someone other than the parents determine how the child should be restricted? If this be the case, at what age of the child should the parent step aside?

I have appreciated the input of many people in this project. Still I fear that many questions remain unanswered. How did the crime of physical child abuse come to encompass any and all forms of parental neglect? Who has the right to determine what constitutes neglect?

How often is neglect determined on the basis of material possession (i.e., the lack of it)? How is it that the same society which so recently criticized permissive parents now demands the right to remove children from a home where parents are thought to be too strict?

The most disturbing question of all concerns the cases in which abuse is suspected. Who should remove the child from the home? When should the child be removed?

The *Miami Herald* reported a case in which three children were removed from a home in which a fourteen-year-old baby sitter was caring for the children. The only message left by the caseworker was to have the parents call in the morning about the children. The parents had no idea where the children were or why they had been taken from the home.

Two Health Rehabilitative Services caseworkers had gone to the home to investigate a child abuse complaint. One of the younger children had two black eyes caused by a fall in the bathroom. The children were whisked off and put in an HRS detention home. The father finally made contact with one HRS department counselor who listened to him. She ordered the children returned to the home but it was only after a thirty-hour ordeal that the reunion took place.

The HRS declares that state law permits caseworkers to enter a home and remove children without parental permission if the worker determines there is a potentially harmful or dangerous situation; however, it is the policy to notify parents immediately. The fact that the parents in this case were not notified is probable cause for an investigation, according to the agency. I imagine this was small comfort to the parents of the children, however.

The criminal is protected in our country, in that no enforcement officer may enter the home of a suspected criminal to search for evidence without a court order. If waiting for such an order impedes the progress of justice, so be it. That is the chance we willingly take in order to avert unwarranted intrusion into the homes of innocent people.

Yet families do not seem to enjoy the same protection from social agencies. Neither the law enforcement officer nor the court has jurisdiction here. Rather, it is the social worker who is charged with investigating the family. No court order is necessary. In most states, one anonymous telephone call is all it takes to send strangers into the home to whisk away the children. And ask questions later.

Handling Conflict with Parental Boundaries

8

Handling Conflict with Parental Boundaries

Official and unofficial outsiders are perhaps too quick to tear down parental boundaries at the first sign of conflict between parent and child. There are sound reasons why the teenager should be encouraged to work through the period of conflict with his parents.

Many people concerned with protecting the rights of youth create open-end situations when teens are presented with options to parental lifestyles. Too many easy options remove the incentive to work through the parental conflict.

Options do not necessarily constitute solutions. An abundance of options causes confusion for the immature. For the teen in conflict with parental values, it is far better to remain in the home, confronting a value with which he does not agree, than to be thrust prematurely into a situation where there is no need to disagree because there are no values.

Avoiding conflict

Several plans for handling parent/teen conflict have been around for quite a while. Plan A is still the favorite: be a perfect parent, raise a perfect child. Thus, there will be no conflict. Since this plan often fails, Plan B must come into play. Plan B calls for pretending that it is not happening to your family.

One man who reviewed my book, *When Parents Cry,* expressed his concern to me that evangelical Christian parents are particularly guilty of Plan B use. Because people do not want to admit to any pain or problems with parent-child relationshps, they relegate this subject to the closet of not-to-be-discussed items.

Plan C calls for throwing in the towel, abdicating responsibilities and trying to survive until the child is gone from home. It is because some parents choose this plan that kids say, "I wish my parents had some rules." Some time ago I read a letter to Ann Landers in which a young boy stated that he was very unhappy because his parents never gave him any guidelines. He wanted rules to live by. He did not appreciate his parents' abdication of their role.

These three plans have two things in common. First, they all approach the problem from the perspective of the parent, and second, none of them is workable.

The latest plan is seen from the perspective of the teen. It isn't workable either. Plan D says the teen in conflict with parents may opt for an escape from all the hassle. In fact, Plan D communicates that the age of hassle is officially over because the teen has the right to seize control of his own life. Get out from under parental restrictions—and no more conflict!

Facing the conflict

The truth is that unless a teen learns how to deal with conflicts with authority, he will never be able to control his own life.

I posed a question to a psychologist who teaches and counsels in the area of the family. "How important is it that the teen work through the period of conflict rather than take one of the legal options?" His answer came in the form of a question, "If not at home, where?"

Where will teens learn to work through conflict with authority if not in the home? Conflict is a lifelong problem. The home is a training ground for life.

Many reasons could be given to support the theory that the teen and parent should work through the period of conflict, but I would like to suggest four.

1. Conflict with authority is a lifelong problem. It concerns me that so many options to solving parent/teen conflicts are available to teens today. If teens are not encouraged to deal with such conflict within the home, how will they handle conflict in other areas of their life?

One does not have to assume that the authority figure must always be right. The boss doesn't have to be right. He only has to be the boss. If he requires his employee to do something which seems "dumb," or a waste of time, that is his prerogative. (If it really is dumb, or a waste of time, it will become *his* problem.)

Ask any employer of teens if he can tell which student has learned to submit to parental authority. Ask if it makes a difference on the job.

When one of our daughters was in her first year of high school she had a problem with a teacher. She was always a charming young girl and for the first time in her life this proved to be a detriment. She found herself in a class taught by a man who could not stand charmers. In fact he bent over backwards to show charmers he could never be affected by charm. With her fragile ego and lack of understanding of the situation, she was soon intimidated by the teacher.

Refusing to ask for help, she nearly failed the subject. When he gave her a poor work warning, she left it in a convenient place for us to find. That was our first knowledge of the problem. Looking into the situation we discovered that there was a definite personality conflict between this teacher and a number of pupils.

What should we have done? Some would say, "Tell the school that they have a problem with the teacher and have her transferred to another class."(They did have a problem. This teacher was not with the school system by the time our daughter graduated.) But my husband and I decided it was to our daughter's best interest if she worked out the conflict with the teacher herself. We hired a tutor for her because without this service she would have failed the course. In addition, we advised her to make every effort to get her work done and to learn how to communicate with the teacher.

"You will meet people all your life who will be in places of authority over you," we told her. "With some of them you are going to have a personality conflict. That's part of life. Learn how to cope with it now."

We believe it was a good learning experience for her. She has proved to be a valuable employee wherever she has worked and we believe that part of her preparation for entering the working world was this initial lesson in dealing with conflicts.

2. *Conflict is never solved by removing oneself from the source.* To be rid of conflict, one must solve it, not run away from it. In a documentary on teens who have run from their conflict, one girl stands out in my memory. At one part of the program she confessed in a highly emotional state that she felt terrible because of the way she had treated her mother.

On many occasions she had said to her mother, "I hate you! I hate you! I hate you!" She had also called her some unprintable names which she could not erase from her memory. When she grew tired of the conflict with her mother, she ran away to a teen shelter. But she had not solved anything. The conflict was still within her.

She would have been better off to have stayed at home. Why? Because Mother is always right? I doubt it. Parents often make mistakes. But one cannot run from inner conflict. It can only be resolved by committing oneself to seeing it through and finding a working relationship.

Our neighbor works with young people in a nationally known organization. One day over lunch he shared with us the background of a girl with whom he had counseled. She is neither abused nor in physical danger but the homelife is not much to brag about. "She gets pretty weary of the situation," he said. "She wanted to run away six months ago, but I persuaded her to stay and see it through. When she has finished school she will be better equipped to be out on her own. In the meantime she may learn something through the experience."

Recently a college freshman shared with me that she

had once had a serious conflict with her father. "I would promise myself that I would not speak to him for three whole days," she told me. I found this hard to believe because theirs is a very close family and she seems especially close to her father.

The problem came during her junior high years and, since they had worked through it so well, I asked, "Suppose that during the height of the problem you had had contact with an adult authority who would have helped you escape all the hassle?" I outlined some of the current options and continued, "What if someone would have been willing to arrange to remove you from your home to escape the conflict with your father?"

She answered, "That is so superficial. How could they know about the family situation just by one conversation? What could they know about my father, or even about me for that matter?" Then she confessed that feelings for her father had fluctuated. One day he was "maybe okay" while the next day she wouldn't speak to him.

3. *By learning to submit to authority, one is prepared to submit to the Supreme Authority.* One of the most important contributions the parent can make to the spiritual training of the child is to teach him to submit to authority. Many important spiritual decisions are based on the ability of the believer to submit himself to God as the Supreme Authority.

In my own life, it is easier to submit my will to God's will because my father taught me to respect authority. We talked about this many years ago. At the time, my mother was dying in a distant hospital. I was married, had three children and lived over 600 miles from my parents. My mother was hospitalized 125 miles from their home. I spent some time with my father during those weeks and every other day or so we would make the long trip to the hospital to visit Mother. This gave us a lot of time for conversation.

As is often the case at such junctures, my father spent a great deal of time verbalizing regrets. One regret was that our mother had borne the responsibility of giving us our spiritual training. My father felt as though he had failed us.

While I had to admit that our basic spiritual training was handled by Mother and that it was through her consistent prayer that each of us had submitted to God's plan for our lives, I was quick to point out to my father that he had made a very significant contribution. "You taught us to obey," I told him, "and because you did, I find it easier to obey the Lord."

In an age of rapidly changing values, the believer must remember that God-given values never change. For the believer, current standards must always be judged against the Word of God. The young person in conflict with parents tends to reject everything the parents stand for, including moral values. But if that young person learns to respect authority, he stands a far greater chance of respecting the authority of God's Word in his life.

It should be the right of the parent and the right of the teen to work through the period of conflict within the confines of the family without intrusion from outside the home. In the semi-controlled environment of the home the teen may hurl new thoughts and strange ideas against what seems to be antiquated moral values. And at some point find a solution.

It is not the end of the world when teens come face to face with the question, "Do I want these to be my values?" Surely at some time in life one must examine values to discover, "Are these really mine or have I simply adopted someone else's standards?'' Only after these questions are answered are personal values of any true benefit.

Lest the reader misunderstand and think that I am advocating that teens be turned loose to seek personal values, let me stipulate this: Anyone, teen or otherwise, who is honestly testing values should be willing to test new thoughts and strange ideas against the Word of God. Every issue must be examined on the basis of the authority of the Scriptures. There should be a concentrated effort by the parents to direct the teen who is questioning values. And it must be remembered that parental values determine the lifestyle of the home and any child still at home must respect those values.

4. There is a reward for working through the conflict. In an article, ''The Real Mother's Day,'' *(Woman's Day,* May, 1974) Eda LeShan declares that the nicest Mother's Day gift she ever received did not come wrapped in fancy ribbons and did not even come on Mother's Day. Her gift came in the middle of the summer when her twenty-three-year-old daughter remarked to her, ''You know the truth is that of all the parents I've met, you and Daddy are the only ones I really respect. You're great.'' The author goes on to describe the emotions she felt at that moment, declaring, ''Despite the date it was suddenly Mother's Day and it remains one of the most moving and thrilling moments of my life.''

I have saved this article for a number of years because I believe the author has shown some significant things for all parents and offspring. The first is that only in retrospect are parents found to be all that great. It is important to remember that 'the daughter who said ''You're great'' was in her twenties at the time. A parent experiences many moments of shared love with the toddler and even with the young child. And many parents testify to an excellent relationship with sons or daughters in their twenties. But between childhood years and the twenties comes something called the teenage years. Most parents will admit that their relationships during those years were not all that great.

Eda LeShan freely acknowledges that she had not been an especially good mother. In her words she was often "... a rotten mother—impatient, ill-tempered, confused, frightened, stupid, childish, insensitive, the full range of human fallibility." There were many times when she regretted having a child. She felt overburdened and under-appreciated. There were crises in her daughter's life which caused this mother to want to die on the spot. There were also lengthy periods when she knew that her daughter regretted being stuck with the author for a mother. At one point the hostility was so great that the mother sat down and wrote an article entitled, "The Year I Became a Monster Mother."

The author emphasizes the need for a loving commitment between parent and child to see the period of conflict through. She sums up motherhood as being trying work but acknowledges that childhood is also full of pain.

All of our daughters are now in their twenties. Not long ago one wrote that she missed us and how thankful she is for having the parents she has. I share that freely because I, like Eda LeShan, was not an especially good mother. I wanted to be. More than anything I wanted to be. But there were times when I failed miserably. Somehow, in retrospect, now that our daughters are in their twenties, they can express confidence in our parenting ability.

Each time a carefully chosen card or a casually spoken word expresses their respect, love and appreciation for us, we give thanks for the joy of being parents. And we have to admit that in retrospect the experience is pretty great, especially for those who commit themselves to working through the conflict.

Combating
Social
Peer
Pressure

9

Combating Social Peer Pressure

The influence of peers during the teenage years is cause for utmost concern because it is during those years that some of life's most important decisions are made. Under peer pressure, decisions may not be made wisely. Decisions are not made by choice, reasoning, or planning but are instead made by compulsion. Under pressure teens may make decisions which set the course of their lives for years to come.

Without question, the protection of parental boundaries must begin by building strong family units. The more the family structure is attacked from without, the stronger it must be from within. Parents cannot look to the school, the church, or the law of the land to enforce boundaries set for their family. If today's youth respect parental authority, it will be because they want to do so. No one is going to force them to obey their parents. No one is going to encourage them to work through their problems at home. Their motivation must come from within. The child who finds security and acceptance in the family unit is more likely to respect parental boundaries.

Importance of family ties

Roots by Alex Haley has been credited with plummeting a record number of people into a frantic search for family roots. Genealogy libraries enjoy new popularity. Adoption records are being searched despite the great expense of time and money required to cut through legal red tape. Personal identity has suddenly become contingent upon family identity.

At the same time the search for family is accelerating, the family unit is being redefined in such a way that blood ties seem to be of no importance. A family unit can be one parent. Or two parents. Or no parents. It can include married couples or unmarried couples. It can house blood-related individuals, or simply a compatible group living together. If a family can be defined so loosely, there seems to be little need to identify the roots from which one has descended.

I find it hard to believe that the traditional family can so easily be redefined out of existence. For all of its problems, the family unit is still vitally important. In spite of a mobile society, in spite of the constant severing of family ties, there is a part of most of us which will always relate best to bloodlines. In times of deepest reflection, it will always be to our childhood that we return. Places, people, events. In our memory they link us to another time and another world.

My own gypsy-like existence has been much like that of the average American. I have enjoyed living in a number of states and several different regions. I have lived in the midwest, the southwest, the Pacific northwest and in both northern and southern California. But in my most melancholy times my thoughts still return to the area where I spent the first ten years of my life.

Being very realistic, I know I could not live there permanently. But it seems essential to my inner peace to return periodically to renew ties with those whom I knew and loved long ago when life was much simpler. Ours is a very large family—150 at a poorly attended reunion. I remember that as a child any gathering of the clan seemed like a holiday no matter what the time of year. With plenty to eat and cousins by the dozens, what more could a child want?

There is no doubt in my mind about the part which the family unit played in shaping my life. The extent of this influence becomes increasingly obvious with each passing year.

My maternal grandmother was a strong and practical individual. Her influence on the family as a whole and upon me as an individual would be hard to measure. In an era when times were hard, she constantly communicated her personal never-give-up philosophy. She did what had to be done and reminded everyone that better times would come.

My father has always credited her with pulling the family through the Depression years. He developed a great admiration for her and I think that she reciprocated with a special place in her heart for him, her only son-in-law. The great esteem with which Father regarded her may be seen in his reaction to an incident which took place the year that she was 83.

Grandmother was on a plane which was hijacked. The captain was shot (he later recovered) but heroic FBI agents felled the hijacker and all the passengers escaped. Unbelievably, at her age and being a woman of no small stature, she was among those who escaped through the window hatch. When my father heard of the incident he quipped, "Had they only known, they would not have needed the FBI. Fritz could have handled it."

My relationship with Fritz was not the grandmother-granddaughter relationship envisioned in grape jelly ads or telephone "reach-out" commercials. Actually she frightened me at times. Yet her superficial severity was balanced by the heartiest, most spontaneous laugh I have ever heard. (Now 93 and without sight, she still laughs easily.)

She taught me many things. But her greatest contribution to my life was the security she gave to us all. As a child I unconsciously accepted what I could not consciously verbalize. Whatever problems came into my world, my parents could handle. And certainly whatever problems were too complicated for them, Fritz could handle.

It is easy to appreciate the value of family ties now at my age. It is significant, however, that some of the strongest opinions regarding the importance of the family unit have been voiced by young people. "Children find security in knowing that at least at home they are accepted and appreciated," said one nineteen-year-old college freshman.

She went on to say that the best thing a parent can do is

to accept a child, spend quality time with him, encourage him and be proud of him. It is not the amount of time the parent spends, she stressed, rather the degree of attention. "You don't say, 'How was your day?' and then go on thinking about something else while they are answering you."

I couldn't help thinking that this girl had expressed all of the vital ingredients which go into building strong family ties.

Peer pressure threatens parental boundaries

Peer pressure has been called the greatest cancer among teenagers today. It may be seen as the first attack upon parental boundaries. It is because of peer pressure that young people begin to reject parental boundaries. Current legislation and social agencies make it easy for young people to reject these boundaries, but peer pressure initiates the action.

In an effort to gain some insight into the problem of peer pressure, I interviewed a family of five. The parents and three children, ages 21, 19 and 16, participated.

I chose this particular family for two specific reasons: (1) They have an excellent family relationship at this time which reflects not a perfect family but a family which has worked through a few problems, and (2) As an army officer's family they have lived in a number of areas and could give input from a wide variety of experiences.

> Girl, 19: "Kids are really looking for acceptance. And that's not just saying, 'I love you,' but saying 'I'm proud of you and I'm interested in what you're doing.' When a child gets acceptance at home, it's so much easier to

face at school not getting acceptance from your friends. When you know you're really accepted at home, at least you've got that going for you."

This participant confirmed what I had suspected for some time. Peer pressure is often strongest at the junior high level. She freely admitted that in junior high she had gone through a lot of experimenting with her friends because she very much wanted to be accepted. The contrast between the friends, who turned out to be back-stabbers, and her family, who gave her acceptance, was a strong factor in the positive outcome of the situation.

Noting that one obvious problem area with peer pressure involves exposure to drugs, I asked, "What, if anything, can a parent do to prevent this?" Their comments revealed first of all that pressure concerning drugs varies from place to place. In some communities the pot-alcohol group does not include academically motivated students. In some communities those involved in drugs and alcohol are from lower income families while in other areas too much money is often a factor.

Speaking on the role of parents, the twenty-one-year-old son reiterated what has been said many, many times.

Boy, 21: "Parents should teach moral lessons when the children are younger, bring them up in a way that's just and teach them the way to live. That's what I think is lacking in parents' lives. They don't have it in their own lives; how are they going to pass something on to their kids?"

I asked if, in the boy's opinion, unstructured upbringing is basically a lack of values on the part of the parents, or a lack of time spent, or both.

> Boy, 21: "For one thing, the kids have too much money—the ones that are into all of these things. Part of it is that the parents don't spend time with children. The kids pick up their role models from TV."

Peer pressure can be a positive influence, as demonstrated by the younger daughter.

> Girl, 16: "The peer pressure is so great in my school for grades, I don't even like to tell anyone if I get a 'C.' Everyone knows they are going to college and they are in there preparing for college entrance."

When asked if she thought the pressure came from parents or from the kids themselves, she responded, "I don't think it's the parents. It's from the kids themselves."

On the whole, however, peer pressure is a negative influence in the life of the child. The fact that it causes him to do things of which his parents disapprove is only part of the problem. Of even greater significance is the fact that peer pressure often causes a child to do things which he does not really enjoy. The activity may seem harmless, yet there is a problem if an activity is initiated solely to avoid rejection by one's peers.

It can hardly be overemphasized that what the child needs most at the point of excessive peer pressure is positive communication that he is accepted by his family.

Anticipating peer pressure

Parents are not always aware of traumatic experiences in a child's life. Parents need to develop a sensitivity to their child. Don't expect the child to call a family conclave and announce, "I am really having a lot of trouble with peer pressure."

Our own daughters faced peer pressure of varied kinds and degrees. After our youngest had shared with us an incident which occurred during her junior high years, her father asked, "Why didn't you tell us?"

She shrugged her shoulders and said, "What could you have done?"

Her father said, "We could have been there."

Sometimes just being there is all that a parent can do and sometimes the parent will not even know what he is being there for. Don't wait for the child to communicate a need.

Be aware that peer pressure starts at an early age and by junior high it is often a serious problem. A well-known Christian educator has been quoted as saying, "The trouble with junior highers is that no one but God loves them." I would differ slightly with that statement in that I think the real trouble with junior highers is that they do not love themselves. Accepting the child at this age and helping him accept himself becomes extremely important if peer pressure is to be combated.

Peer pressure will affect different personalities to varying degrees. The strong-willed child may end up poking some peer in the nose rather than capitulating to some unpleasant pressure, while the more docile child may easily give in to the crowd.

Perhaps most important of all, remember that self-esteem is the best deterrent to peer pressure. In his cassette series, "Self Esteem For Your Child," Dr. James Dobson says that the child who is most inferior in his own eyes is in the greatest danger in terms of his own vulnerability. Feelings of inferiority impose conformity upon our children, according to Dobson. This is the cause of much conflict, including sexual pressures. This feeling of inferiority is what makes the teen feel that virginity is something to get rid of before someone finds out about it.

Dobson believes that the Christian has the key to self-esteem and explains that it comes from one place—not from achievement, not from possessions, not from race, but from human acceptance. Furthermore, he expresses the opinion that Jesus Christ puts a high priority on our responsibility to be a giving, loving and caring people.

The parent should begin early in the child's life to build self-esteem. Self-esteem is never attained through reaching an older brother's or sister's standards. Self-esteem is developed as the child learns that he is accepted as an individual with his own special contribution to make in the family and in the world.

The extent of peer pressure

Just how widespread is the problem of peer pressure? A CBS Special Report with Harry Reasoner explored the question. Regarding teenage sexual habits, the question was posed, "Does peer pressure affect the decision to become sexually active?" It was interesting to note that even when the respondent answered, "Not really," the fact which always came out was, "Everybody's doing it."

Writing in the *Chicago Tribune,* Jack Mabley quoted Dr. Rhoda Lorand, a practicing psychotherapist, who takes a different approach to the subject of teen sex. Dr. Lorand feels it is an illusion of sex educators and family planners that young girls engage in sex out of desire. She maintains that passion is conspicuously absent, and peer pressure is seen as the motivating factor—everybody's doing it. Instead of distributing contraceptives, Dr. Lorand suggests that family planning agencies might better provide counseling to help children resist peer pressure and acquire an independent sense of worth.

Applying parental pressure

My husband and I once served on a panel with Dr. Bob Warren, a well-respected minister and father of two grown girls. One question addressed to the panel was, "How do you explain to teenagers why they can't do everything their friends do?" Bob explained it best. "I always told my daughter, 'You can't do that because your name is Warren and your friend's name is Smith. And the Warren family has a different standard than the Smith family.'"

My husband often reminded our girls, "Remember who you belong to." In our case that meant, "You belong to the Gage family and you belong to Jesus Christ." I think that it is good to remind a child to whom he belongs and to do everything possible to make him secure in that position.

When my sister and I were growing up we shared the same room. For Christmas one year, our mother gave us a framed copy of a poem to hang on our wall. That poem now hangs on the wall of the Gage home beside the framed photos of three girls. Many people have read it, most have admired it and some have copied it. I am sorry to say that the poet's name is nowhere on the copy so I cannot give credit. Nevertheless I submit it here as a closing thought for this chapter.

114

To My Daughters

Do you know that you are my own little girls
To mother the dearest thing in all the world,
The joy of my life, the pride of my heart,
Of my very soul and being a part?
When in coming years, we drift apart
The memory of Mother keep close to your heart.
Remember the world in honoring you
Will honor, dear heart, your mother too.

Combating Economic Peer Pressure

10

Combating Economic Peer Pressure

Teaching young people to resist economic peer pressure is an integral part of parental training. If peer pressure cannot be resisted at the economic level, there is little chance that it will be resisted at the social and other levels.

Keeping up with the Joneses is another name for economic peer pressure. Giving in to economic peer pressure may be accurately described as the act of buying what you do not want with money you do not have to impress people you do not like.

The effects of such spending may be seen in an inflated economy which presupposes two wage earners for every household. Misuse of credit, too much hypertension and too little peace of mind are a few of the problems which accompany submission to economic peer pressure.

Obviously, if a parent is to teach a child to avoid such pressures the parent must be in control of his own finances. This demands decisiveness. It always takes courage to spend your time, your money and your life the way you think best, without regard to how you may or may not impress someone else. For those who need help in assuming control of finances, there are several good books including, *It Only Hurts Between Paydays* by Amy Ross Mumford, Accent Books, Denver, Colorado.

Much of what a child learns concerning economics will be absorbed through observing parental attitudes and spending habits. In addition, the child should be taught specific monetary principles.

Beginning at an early age, teach your child that money may be spent anyway he likes but it may be spent only once. If the child squanders his entire allowance the first hour, let him enjoy this brief tycoon experience, but let him go without spending money until his next allowance.

As soon as the child has learned a measure of responsibility with his spending money, he should be taught the principle of budgeting money for necessities and for pleasure. The earlier the child learns to do this, the better.

In our family, the most effective teaching tool for the preceding principles proved to be the way in which we handled the weekly allowance. Our circumstances never permitted large allowances, but we always allotted some from the budget for this purpose. To this allowance we added whatever monies the child needed for the week for lunches, Sunday School offering, and other needs. Early in life our children learned to set aside money to cover necessities.

Media pressure

Teaching children to handle money is not without problems. The media quickly spreads the word on what everyone else in the world is driving, wearing, or doing. The affluence to which our youth is exposed is coercive. Yet many, perhaps most, of them cannot have what is daily dangled before them. Subsequently, exposure to such affluence becomes a negative influence in their lives. Young people soon begin to add up all the things they think they are missing.

This past year we moved to Marin County, California. Marin County has been the subject of several network specials, not a few books and a recent movie. It has come to be characterized as a place where people are completely self-centered, grabbing all that gives pleasure and caring for little else but material possessions. Supposedly peacock feathers, hot tubs and the slogan, "I want it all now," reign.

The fact that Marin has the best of all possible worlds (secluded countryside with beautiful rolling hills located a few minutes from downtown San Francisco) is rarely mentioned. Nor does the outside world take note of the fact that Marin is populated by highly motivated people.

When we came to Marin we found the image projected by the media a little less than accurate. We found merchants to be the most congenial we have met anywhere. We found the people delightful. We met affluent parents who are concerned that their children not grow up having too much too soon. We saw affluent believers using their money in unusual ways to share their faith in Jesus Christ.

We have come to feel at home in this county of high achievers where most speak a language foreign to us because they live in a world of computer technology and high finances and we have problems balancing the checkbook.

The parents' attitude toward possessions is of utmost importance in teaching a child to resist the media. No matter what the media says the rest of the world has, if the parents demonstrate a proper perspective toward possessions, they have won the first round.

Certainly it isn't always easy. I can remember many times in my own life when I wished for some of the things which seemed reserved for people of status. But, as someone so succinctly put it, the trouble with status symbols is that by the time you can afford them you no longer need them. They are simply not that important.

Living within your means

Because a pastor's salary is usually limited, I had to learn to manage our finances rather strictly. No one wants a pastor who is always in debt (not even churches which do not pay an adequate salary). Thus, I had a built-in incentive for resisting economic peer pressure.

There are other incentives which are less binding but just as important. I remember reading a story about a banker's family. The son was overheard one day telling a friend, "We can't afford that."

The friend was so shocked that the banker father stepped in and explained an important principle regarding family finances.

"What he means is that we have other places to put our

money," explained the father. Those other places included savings and college funds which, for the time being, precluded using the money for many other things.

For some couples, resisting economic peer pressure may mean living on one salary instead of two. Mothers who choose to stay home often do so with the knowledge that the budget will be tight. There are many reasons why a mother may choose to go to work, but if the primary reason is to supply all the extras that others have, it is a good sign that the parents have lost the battle of economic pressure from their own peers.

For those who determine to live on one salary, it often means a different lifestyle, setting different priorities. It means buying end-of-year sale items, sewing (whether you enjoy it or not), using in-season produce, and fixing the cheapest meat a hundred different ways.

Living within your means often means not having everything you want. But we may rest assured that we are in good company in this respect. One of the richest men in America was once asked, "If you could have anything you wanted, what would it be?" The man replied, "Just a little more money."

For years we had a newspaper clipping on our bulletin board. A store had adopted the slogan, "If we don't have it, or can't get it, you don't want it." To this I added Philippians 4:19. It served as a reminder that, while God has promised to supply all our needs, that does not necessarily cover all our wants.

The challenge of the teenage wardrobe

One of the greatest problem areas of economic peer pressure usually presents itself at the end of the summer when parents begin to think about back-to-school clothes. What is IN this year? And what is OUT? And woe to the parent who insists that the child wear what is OUT.

Since we had no boys I do not know to what extent this hits them or at what age. But with our girls it seemed that the onset of the wardrobe problems always came at junior high age. The most effective tool we found for dealing with the problem was once again the allowance. This time it was a clothing allowance.

Our firstborn was still a baby when I read about a mother who had solved a major conflict over clothes with her teenager through a clothing allowance plan. We were so impressed with the plan that we determined that when the time came we would endeavor to use it. I believe variations of the plan will work for any family in virtually any economic bracket.

Basically, this is how it works. First determine the approximate amount of money spent on clothing for the child in question over a one-year period. Divide by 52; this gives the weekly clothing allowance for the child. Never apologize if it is not a substantial sum. Simply tell the child, "This is your share of what we as a family are able to spend on clothing. You may spend it any way you want, but remember, you will have to live with your decisions. Make sure that you like what you buy, and that it will last." (Obviously if you have not given basic training in spending habits before this juncture, you may be in for some problems.)

The most frequently-asked question concerning this plan is, "What if the child brings home something which you consider indecent or in poor taste for the intended occasion?" We cautioned the girls to exercise good judgment and we reserved the right to disapprove purchases which failed to meet family standards.

I often went shopping with the girls, giving advice or helping to evaluate potential purchases. The final decisions, however, were entirely up to them.

A personal clothing budget affected their attitudes toward purchases immediately. They began to look more closely at the latest fad. On their limited budget they could not afford an item which would be out of style long before they outwore or outgrew it. Charles Schulz captured the gist of this problem in a "Peanuts" cartoon. Charlie Brown says that the dumbest thing his grandfather ever did was not finish high school. But the smartest thing he ever did was that he never bought a Neru jacket.

The girls soon became critics of quality. When it was their own money, they learned to take a close look at construction, care instructions, and wear potential, as well as style.

As a result of the clothing allowance, it suddenly became acceptable to wear altered clothing, including hand-me-downs. We have laughed over one incident which is indicative of what shouldering economic responsibility can do.

One of our daughters had been given a pair of jeans, in good shape, but too big. She felt it somehow demeaning to wear those jeans, even though I had suggested that she allow me to alter them for her. The jeans were still lying around the day we decided to start her on a clothing allowance. The first thing she said as she left the room was, "Well, it's all up to me now. Where did I put those jeans? I can save a lot of money if I take those in and wear them."

The rewards of doing without nonessentials

Several times I have participated in workshops dealing with economics in the parsonage. One thing I like to share is that there is a distinct advantage in learning to do without nonessentials. Eventually, with good management, you will find that you can afford some of those things. But by that time you may decide that you don't want the item and you can use the money for something else.

As an example, for years living within our means meant having only one car and having a portable black and white television. By the time we could afford a second car or another television, we couldn't think of any reason to spend our money that way. Instead of buying the car or a color television we took a family trip to Europe.

The two daughters who were still at home made the trip with us. One daughter was in her last semester of high school with only one class per day. She was working full time and planning for college in the fall. She paid her own way. The younger daughter, too young to work, saved her own spending money.

Going to Europe, Arthur Frommer style (Europe on $15 per day), takes a lot of planning and cooperation from each family member. But for us, there has been no greater family experience because it was something which we really wanted to do.

In many ways the trip proved to be a learning experience for the girls. During the final days of preparation some of their friends learned of our summer plans and commented on the expense of such a trip. When the girls shared the comments we had a good opportunity to discuss the subject of economics.

"How many of your friends have two cars in the

family?''

"All of them. Some have one for every driver."

"For the price of one old klunker, one person can go to Europe."

"How many have a large color television?"

"All of them. Most have two."

Our discussion had nothing to do with the merits of traveling as opposed to owning more than one car. Travel isn't for everyone. Our discussion concerned the principle we had endeavored to teach them since childhood: Money can be spent any way you like. But it can be spent only once.

On January 16, 1980, gold peaked at a high of $770 per ounce. The next evening our newspaper carried an article suggesting at least twenty ways to spend $770 if you did not happen to have gold fever.

Among options suggested in this tongue-in-cheek article: dinner for four at a New York restaurant, rental of a Rolls Royce for twenty hours, purchasing a secondhand car, or Xerox or Litton stocks.

A final thought on resisting peer pressure is drawn from another tongue-in-cheek article from our local newspaper. In "Kids as Fashion Snobs," writer Win Murphy takes a facetious look at the problem. "A friend of mine has a kid in kindergarten," writes Murphy, "who campaigned for $22 jeans and refused to wear her 'yucky' elastic-waisted corduroy pants to school.

"The mom gave in. 'You've lost the war before you fired even one cannon,' I complained to her. 'By the time that kid's in first grade she'll be demanding Gucci underwear and personal haircuts by Vidal Sassoon and you'll be scrounging the thrift stores to buy yourself a blouse.'

" 'Well,' the mother reasoned, 'she just wants to be

like her little friends.' "

Murphy's final comment: "It's that kind of vicious circle that has parents pulling their hair out when the bills come in and keeps the clothes designers smiling from ear to ear—year to year."

I believe that one of the easier battles for the parents to win is the battle against economic peer pressure. When the parent takes the trouble to give the child proper training, I believe a special kind of strength is instilled in the child. The ability to withstand economic peer pressure will encourage the child to be his own person. This will, in turn, help the child to withstand peer pressure at other levels of life.

Parental Support Through the Pulpit Ministry

11

Parental Support Through the Pulpit Ministry

Parents should never relegate total spiritual training of the child to the church. Parents who have no interest in spiritual matters are often accused of this practice, but the Christian parent who regularly attends church is also guilty. It may not be quite so obvious, but he is guilty nevertheless.

Many Christian parents feel that after they have paid their tithe, served on a few committees, taught a class and campaigned to call a good youth pastor, their responsibility is over. The church should reciprocate by taking charge of the spiritual development of their children, especially their teenage children. If anything goes wrong it becomes the pastor's fault, the church's fault or the youth pastor's fault.

Parents cannot abdicate their spiritual responsibility to their children. They cannot lay this task upon the church in general or the pastoral staff in particular. Parents should, however, be able to expect a strong support system from within the church.

The local church can provide a support system for the family in four basic areas: through the pulpit ministry; through a proper attitude of the congregation at large; through family-oriented programming; and through a sensitive youth ministry.

Underscoring moral training

No church can provide an adequate support system for the family today unless the pulpit ministry includes preaching against the social evils of the day. When the family is struggling to survive, when parents are endeavoring to maintain boundaries for their children, they need a pulpit ministry which will underscore the moral training given in the home.

My husband knew he was in a new ballpark, ministry-wise, the first time he counseled with an eighteen-year-old girl who did not know there was anything wrong with premarital sex.

My husband and I grew up in a generation where the population of our respective worlds could be divided into three groups. The churched people were on one side and the nonchurched people with low morals on the other side.

In between there was a buffer group with high morals

but no church affiliation. We have lived to see the buffer group disappear. Lines are no longer distinct. People with few moral convictions are now among the regular attenders at some of America's most evangelical churches. In fact, they are even seeking to serve within these churches.

Doug was a young man who had experience in children's work. When he moved to a new town he immediately began to attend church. Soon he volunteered to get involved in a children's ministry. The pastor turned him down because Doug was living with his girlfriend.

Both Doug and his friend were from Christian homes. They had rationalized their situation until they saw nothing about their unmarried state which would be incompatible with a ministry in their local church.

Such situations are not uncommon. Aside from handling each problem as it arises, what can the minister do to counteract the trend?

Rev. James Dobson, Sr., in the book *Family Under Fire* (Beacon Press, 1976) by his son, Dr. James Dobson, has said, "When a minister presents only the love of God, he makes it impossible for his congregation to understand the purpose of Jesus' life and death. The Messiah came to provide a remedy for a disease. That disease is called sin. If people are not taught the awful, vile nature of man's sinful state and God's hatred for it, then it is impossible for them to comprehend the miraculous remedy made available on the cross."

It seems most incongruous to me that in an age of rising immorality there has been a decline in preaching on that old-fashioned word, separation. Second Corinthians 6:17,18 declares, "Therefore come out from among them, and be ye separate, saith the Lord. . . ." Sometimes it almost seems as if the contemporary Christian is unaware of the fact that there really is a negative side to Christianity.

Presenting the negative side of positive Christianity

Positive Christian truths have been embraced in a folksy approach to the Heavenly Father which totally obscures the negative principles for Christian living. The central truth which has emerged in this lopsided teaching is that God loves us with a wonderful but undemanding love, and the believer's response to such love does not necessarily include a turning away from former habits, desires, or associates.

Consequently, we have a new generation of believers who are largely ignorant of anything called a separated lifestyle. Such a philosophy affects children of Christian parents and tends to widen the communication gap between parent and child.

No doubt the philosophy came about through a reaction of the masses against the legalistic approach to Christian living under which the over-forty generation grew up. Certainly that approach deserved some serious scrutiny. But as is usually the case, in reacting against one extreme the reactionary has embraced another extreme. He has erroneously interpreted Christian liberty as the right of the individual to do whatever he wants.

One young leader adamantly stated, "So long as my conscience is clear before the Lord, what business is it of anyone else what I do?" Ten thousand adherents to such a self-centered philosophy will never make it biblical. The Scriptures clearly teach that we have a responsibility to the conscience of other believers.

Christian love not a panacea

The contemporary Christian regards Christian love as a panacea for every problem. Even his definition of love is evidence of current confusion. "You stab me in the back and I'll wipe the knife off before handing it back to you," is one contemporary explanation of Christian love. Translated, that means, "No matter what you do or whom you hurt, I will be quiet and love you. That will show you that I am a real Christian. In reverse, I expect you to accept me as I am without question and without judgment, no matter what I do."

Such a philosophy tends to erase absolutes and generates strange extremes in behavior. The individual's conscience then becomes the norm for Christian conduct. This is neither sensible nor is it scriptural. The strongest case against this approach is the Book of Judges. This divine recording details the consequences of every man doing what is right in his own eyes.

Doing right by forsaking wrong

Doing what is right in God's eyes has always involved forsaking evil. As the parent endeavors to instruct the child in sound moral principles he will find encouragement from a minister who teaches this truth.

Sometimes it appears we have forgotten the connection between turning from evil in order to do good. Almost without realizing it the believer slips into the pattern of accepting good acts as a balance to evil in one's life. One of the most comprehensive passages concerning the Christian life may be found in Titus 2:11-14. Here the Apostle Paul speaks of denying ungodliness and worldly lusts. To deny involves forsaking and turning away. One must turn away from and take a stand against the thing denied.

Recognizing truth

Before one can deny ungodliness, he must be able to recognize it. While the world is rationalizing evil, promoting emotionally-charged crusades and applying pressure through propaganda, the Christian must learn to think clearly. What is right? What is wrong? The liberated and the sophisticated are crying for the acceptance of homosexual and promiscuous lifestyles as legitimate and respectable. Whatever label men may affix, it is still wrong when God has labeled it thus.

In denying ungodliness, one must deny ungodly doctrine as well as ungodly living. Again, before it can be denied it must be recognized. Today, cults and sects are amassing converts in record numbers. False doctrine is being condoned on every hand because Christians are confused, unlearned and unwilling to make the effort involved in serious Bible study.

The pulpit ministry is of utmost importance if the trend is to be reversed. Believers must be warned against embracing every movement which proclaims devotion to Jesus. They must be alerted to the fact that the deceived can be devout and the devout can be deceived.

On the other hand, minor differences must be put aside in the interest of Christian unity. To do this, the believer must be able to separate the scripturally wrong from that which is religiously condemned. He must concede that which needs to be changed and consistently refuse to change that which must remain constant.

Fortunate indeed is the congregation whose minister leads the people in discovering biblical answers to moral problems. In particular, such a ministry is a blessing to the parent who is endeavoring to guide a teenager through difficult times.

The congregational attitude

Aside from a strong pulpit ministry, the attitude of the congregation as a whole will determine the extent to which the church provides a support system for the parent.

Louis is a young man who has come through a drug addiction even though he grew up in church. During the time that drugs were complicating his life he continued to attend church with his Christian parents. He was surly, rebellious and incommunicative.

In the congregation were two older men (who had been grandparents long before drugs became a nationwide problem) who were able to empathize with Louis' parents. Each made it a point to talk to Louis, even when he was obnoxious.

Through a series of events which the Lord used in Louis' life, he got straightened around.

Supportive people will more easily be found in those churches whose members look upon themselves as a family unit. In a sense they must see the children of other members as their own nieces and nephews. When such a family spirit is cultivated, the family in trouble is more likely to feel supported in a crisis.

In more than twenty-five years in the ministry I am sure there were many people in our congregations who prayed for our children. But only one man took it upon himself to tell me. I shall never forget the encouragement I felt when he said to me, "The Lord has laid it upon my heart to pray for your children every day."

Our children were all still at home and there were no major problems confronting us. It was just that he realized that if we were all members of one family, he had a certain responsibility toward my children.

Right answers and wrong problems

Not all people are as perceptive or as compassionate as those who took an interest in Louis and in our children. Also, some are not very well informed. To understand problems facing families today one must stay informed. It is fruitless to have all the answers if you are unaware of the questions being asked.

I am sometimes reminded of an experience my husband had while teaching school. One day one of his favorite little third grade girls handed in a very strange math paper. She had all the right answers on the page. But from problem three on, those answers were aligned with the wrong problems.

One glance at the paper revealed that Karen had discovered the answers in the back of the book and had proceeded to copy them. After copying the first two answers she had become confused and for the remainder of the paper she had all the right answers with all the wrong problems.

Just because the church has the answer book, it does not follow that all the problems will be solved. Ministers, lay teachers and parents may be skilled in providing answers. But unless they are addressing current problems, most of the questions will remain unanswered.

Protecting parental boundaries is first the responsibility of the parent. But for the Christian parent, the task becomes less complicated if the church provides a strong support system.

Parental Support Through the Church Program and Personnel

12

Parental Support Through the Church Program and Personnel

The role of the church as it relates to the family should be kept in perspective. It should not be misconstrued or exaggerated to the extent that the church is seen as a cure-all for the problems which the family faces.

Many people simply do not realize to what extent they place the responsibility of caring for their problems upon the church. The ministry of the youth pastor is thought to be the magic end to all problems with rebelling youth. The program of the church is seen to be an all-encompassing plan to meet the total needs of the corporate body. Anything less means a failure of the church to be a relevant institution.

More family awareness

On the other hand, the church plays a significant part in the struggle to protect parental boundaries. The survival of the family should be among the primary concerns of the church today.

The church which provides a parental support system will have a program which allows for some family-oriented activities and personnel who, while ministering to individual age groups, will be supportive of the family unit.

So much of the weekly church calendar is segmented by age—children's choir on Monday, junior nature hike on Tuesday, junior high party on Wednesday, ladies' meeting on Thursday, youth night on Friday and men's breakfast on Saturday. Somewhere on the calendar there need to be regularly scheduled events for families. The more parent-child participation these events encourage, the better.

Shortly after moving to our present location my husband and I attended a family Olympic night sponsored by our Christian school. Parents, teamed with their children, competed against other parents and their children. This was one of the most fun-filled family events I have ever witnessed. The entire evening was planned by a parents' committee. The idea could easily be adapted for a church family night.

A family camp and an annual family picnic are among the other events we have been pleased to find on our church calendar. Sunday School picnics and church camps are nothing new, but a family style picnic means families come together. The church bus does not go around and pick up the children, leaving parents at home. Family camping provides unforgettable experiences for the children. (Admittedly it is hard on the older generation!)

The church doesn't have to take charge of the family social needs, but in a day when the family tends to do nothing together except sleep in the same house, the church should allow for and encourage family events. The church has long been sensitive to needs of various subgroups—singles, single parents, senior citizens. But there is a point where the division by age, interests and hobbies must give way to events which are geared toward families having fun together.

Good personnel-family relations

The most crucial problems for the family seeking support from the church may come in the personnel department. In addition to the senior pastor, churches now employ family counselors, youth ministers and other specialized persons. Proper training and experience are seen to be fundamental qualifications for their positions. The success of the personnel, however, is likely to be determined by their attitude toward the people who make up the church.

A sensitive youth minister can be a positive influence, but it should be remembered that he has the potential for a negative influence as well. When the youth minister sees the youth as part of their family unit as well as part of the church family, he will communicate his support for the family. On the other hand, a youth minister who treats the youth as a separate group apart from family or church can be divisive to the family, of little lasting value to the church program, and a potential negative influence to the church.

The youth minister may not work directly with parents but he must be aware of their opinions, desires, likes and dislikes. When certain mores are changing he should be careful about taking upon himself the work of bringing about change. In matters of moral standards he must be aware of and uphold the various attitudes represented within the church.

Encourage submission to parents

One youth minister remarked concerning a problem, "I don't see anything wrong with what Jerry wants to do."

"Neither do I," said an older Christian, "except for one thing."

"And what is that?" asked the youth pastor.

"His father does not approve," replied the older Christian.

Any counseling regarding family standards must reflect a respect for the biblical principle, "Obey your father and mother." The family standard may seem overly strict to the youth minister and he may not find any other principle to support it; but where minor young people are involved, the issue is never just movies, proms or music. The issue is family support and parental boundaries. Neither the church in general nor the youth pastor in particular should pose yet one more threat to those boundaries.

Some would suggest that an effective means of skirting the problem of promoting an event objectionable to some of the parents would be to advise the young people,

"Don't participate in this event if your parents object." This is hardly a solution. The teen is then put in the position of feeling peer pressure from the youth group. This in turn puts him in conflict with his parents. No young person should have to experience negative peer pressure from this source. Nor should parents have to experience a threat to the unity of the family from the church.

No church can act as a support system for the family as long as its program or its personnel promote activities which violate parental convictions. Doing so directly challenges the principle of submission to parental authority.

The role of the seminary

When complications arise in the personnel-parent relations, my sympathies often lie as much with the youth pastors as with the church families. It would seem that schools training young seminarians could do more to emphasize the fact that no matter what training the student receives, his ministry will rise or fall on his ability to relate to and communicate with people. For the youth minister that means relating to parents and the other adults as well as to the youth.

It seems incredible to me that a seminary graduate specializing in youth work would fail to recognize the importance of developing rapport with parents. Parents are not impressed with how much the youth pastor knows or how many degrees he has. They have very little concept of his worth on the job market because of those degrees. Parents only relate to one narrow area: How does he get along with my kids, and does he have to undermine me to gain their confidence?

Ministering to both parent and teen

Counseling high school youth sometimes puts the youth minister in an awkward position. He must, of course, have the teens' confidence. Teens need to feel that they can talk to him without having everything repeated to Mom or Dad. The teen years are years of great conflict. Young people need confidants. But the skilled counselor can easily listen and advise without undermining the parent. Supportive counseling is a sensitive area which demands serious preparation in terms of job skills. It also demands much prayer on the part of the counselor.

One of the most helpful things a youth minister can do for the parent is to provide current information on problems which teens encounter daily. A number of years ago I attended a seminar for youth workers, high school teachers, and others who work with teens. Upon entering the room I noted that the crowd ranged in age from about 25 to 75. The seminar was to be conducted by two young youth ministers. Skeptically I expected to be flooded with the latest innovations, terminology, and "Do's and Don'ts" for parents.

I was pleasantly surprised with the first words of the leader. After surveying the group, he remarked that there were probably many things he could learn from some in the audience. It was obvious they were old enough to have already raised a family while he was just beginning.

He then explained that his role was not to tell us what to do as much as to apprise us of current problems faced by youth. The hour passed quickly as he outlined social issues which confronted teenagers on their high school campuses. It was one of the most helpful seminars I have ever attended.

It would be well if such seminars could be given periodically in local churches. Unless adults are aware of what is going on in the teenage world, they cannot possibly appreciate the problems encountered by families today. Without such information some adults will find it difficult to be supportive of parents with problem kids. Neither will an uninformed person be able to pray specifically for the kids with problems.

I once related to an audience of retirees some of the legal problems facing parents today who try to impose control on their children. The group could not conceive of a world in which Dad's word is not always law. They found it hard to believe that forces outside the home may challenge parental authority. Thus, keeping adults who do not have teenagers informed of pressures confronting teens and their parents is an important part of a sensitive youth ministry.

The church and sex education

It has been suggested that the church could offer a worthwhile service by training parents to handle sex education in their own homes with their own children.

Several reasons have been given to support the idea. One psychologist with many years' experience in family counseling expressed fear that it may be too late to control what is taught in public schools. Although parents must remain alert and do everything possible to shelve objectionable material in public classrooms, they must also recognize that this is not the total answer.

Nor did this counselor see the Christian school as a total answer. Not every child is going to have this opportunity. Thus, the need for strong parental teaching in the home arises. This teaching is seen as a counterattack by parents to public school teaching. In terms of protecting parental boundaries, as in other areas of life, the best defense is a good offense!

There are many ways in which the church can aid parents who need help in providing sex education in the home. Carefully planned seminars, visiting speakers, available visuals and a library for use by the parents are a few.

The programs offered should encourage parental input. Training parents to train their children presents fewer problems than trying to directly train the children.

In a word—communicating

Whatever the program, whatever the curriculum, the church interested in youth will show a genuine interest in the total family. Encouraging communication between parent and teen is best done by demonstrating the ability to communicate with both generations. In an age when the family unit is being threatened on every hand it is my deep prayer that churches will stand as a firm support for the family.

Rebuilding
Broken
Lives

13

Rebuilding
Broken Lives

For the most part, protecting parental boundaries will continue to be a subject involving many unanswered questions, unresolved problems and incomplete solutions.

The best defense for a parent is to build a strong family unit and seek support from within his church. Yet these are only partial solutions.

In spite of every attempt a parent makes to equip a child to withstand peer pressure, some are going to find it easier to go with the flow. With the aid of a third party, some will opt for an early escape from parental boundaries. So long as this option is readily available there will be no real answers for the parents' dilemma.

Teenage conflict with parental boundaries is a family matter. Unless that conflict results in the commission of a crime, it should remain a family matter. Neither government nor schools, neither family planning clinics nor social agencies, should intervene in the conflict. Options to working through the conflict should not be offered. Parental boundaries should not be broken by anyone other than parent or child. Until society recognizes this, the job of the parent will become increasingly complicated.

The parents' role in mending broken lives

How does the parent help his child to mend a broken life? Teaching right from wrong is a preventive measure. So is building strong family units. And becoming involved in a strong, supportive church. But what of those hundreds of thousands for whom a prevention message is now useless? What of those who have lost their virginity? What of those eight million women (many adolescents) who know the guilt of aborting their children?

Rebuilding broken lives demands a forgiving, loving and compassionate attitude on the part of those who seek to aid in the rebuilding. Helping an adolescent pick up the pieces of a broken life demands forgiveness and sacrificial love from the parent. The family name may have been blemished; the parents' hearts may have been broken. But the parents who have experienced the forgiveness of a Heavenly Father can scarcely withhold forgiveness from their own child.

Second, a parent should bear in mind that the greater

the guilt, the worse the child may act. This is especially true if the child is put in the position of covering up his actions. This multiplies the problem by adding lying, subterfuge, and deceit to other negative actions. If the child is a believer, he realizes these actions constitute sin. If he continues covering up sin, his actions may result in hardened attitudes.

Even when he tires of the mess he's made of his life, the child will not always be able to verbalize his feelings. No matter how desperate he is for help, he may need to be confronted kindly with his need before he will discuss it. This act of confrontation demands wisdom on the part of the parent. I believe that a parent who is sensitive to his child and who practices praying for guidance will be able to discern the best time for such a confrontation.

Third, the parent should understand that a certain amount of verbalizing may have to take place before the child can accept forgiveness. The child may want to spill out everything once the subject is opened. Or he may have little to say at the initial confrontation, but the door is open for a continuing dialogue about the problem.

The overindulgent parent who is tempted to cover personal hurt will probably impede spiritual healing. It is better at this point to be gently honest. "We were so hurt, but we never stopped loving you."

Expressing love to a child after everything is out in the open has a special meaning. The rug has been turned over, all the hidden things (or things thought to be hidden) are known to the parent. The parent has acknowledged hurt and expressed love. The child has acknowledged his actions. This is the time to offer forgiveness in addition to love.

Encouraging the Christian adolescent to seek God's forgiveness is the next natural step for the parent. The child who has expressed regret openly should certainly be directed to confess his sins to God, and then to receive God's forgiveness and go on with his life.

For a number of years it has been of special concern to me that Christian adolescents find it particularly difficult to receive God's forgiveness after they have made a mess of their lives. In our experience we have found that this is not a problem for young people who spent years in debauchery, then found Christ as Saviour and Lord. For them, their act of receiving Christ washed away the past with all of its guilt.

However, it is different with the adolescent who grew up in the church, received Christ at an early age and then succumbed to peer pressure. For this young person who has grieved the heart of Saviour and parent alike, the road back is often much more difficult. Such young people need to know God's forgiveness and His sustaining power for the future. As the parent reaches out in love, one of his primary aims should be to lead the child to accept Christ's forgiveness.

The church's role

Some time ago, as I was preparing to speak to a group of about 500 people representing several generations, I was confronted with the thought that the church can no longer present a message which is solely preventive in nature. Statistics show that in a group the size to which I would be speaking, there were a number for whom preventive theology would now be too late. Their troubled consciences would need a message which presented forgiveness and the way back to a spiritually productive life.

What can the church do? Certainly the pulpit ministry

plays a strategic role. Preaching against social evils of the day must be accompanied by exhortation to repentance by believers.

The general attitude of the congregation will determine to what extent the repentant believer will enjoy fellowship within the church. Congregations tend to vacillate between the overly permissive ("I don't think we should judge anyone else.") and the overly judgmental ("You are absolutely wrong."). Neither position is scripturally correct.

There are scriptural principles for taking a hard line on certain sins, including many of which are rampant among liberated youth. Some sins must be judged by putting the guilty out of the assembly. But the congregation must remember that the purpose of such judgment is to bring the guilty one to a place of repentance and then to restore him to fellowship. The congregation must be willing to receive the repentant. Nothing should be done to condone sin. But neither should the repentant one be denied forgiveness and restoration.

Practical aid is another way in which the church may minister to people with broken lives. Some churches are taking creative approaches toward this type of ministry. In Washington, D.C., where abortions outnumber live births, two Virginia churches are sponsoring the nation's first crisis pregnancy center. Staffed by both black and white counselors, the center counsels pregnant women to bring unborn children to term. Poor women who decide to keep their children are referred to "shepherding homes" where they live with a family while waiting for the birth of their child. Organizing such centers is one part of the ministry of the Christian Action Council, a Washington-based evangelical service.

In other areas, Christians man hot lines to aid in solving family problems. The hot line counselor often provides much needed practical aid to a repentant person.

A friend who was once a heroin addict related to us that after he became a Christian he had the very real problem of dealing with his addiction. Three young friends took it upon themselves to stay with him round the clock for the better part of a week. They stayed with him through every ugly scene, and with their help his broken life was put back together again.

Society's role

It is difficult for people to be objective about parental boundaries. As humans we tend to be selective in our support of anything, disregarding principles and supporting only that with which we agree. Asking a group, "Should parents be supported in the boundaries they set for minors?" will likely get an immediate "Absolutely" if that group consists of parents.

But the same group will usually be somewhat less positive where specific cases of parent-teen conflict are outlined. Such information tends to divide the group. Those who agree with the parents' decision will agree that parental boundaries should be supported. Those who disagree with the parents' decision will be less supportive. And the basic principle is lost somewhere in the debate.

I have yet to meet a parent with whom I agreed on every point of child rearing. (I suspect that I have yet to meet one who agrees with me point by point.) But that does not keep me from supporting his right to set boundaries as his conscience dictates.

Such support is too often lacking in our society. For this reason, the parent in conflict with a minor over boundaries may feel quite alone much of the time.

The parent will continue to regard with suspicion many persons who profess to have the best interest of teens at heart. Particularly, he will find it hard to accept advice from an individual who has done everything except raise a teenager and who has been everywhere except up all night waiting for a son to come home. Being fiercely protective of his child, the parent readily sees that protecting the rights of the child is not the same as protecting the child.

A life made whole

For the child who has prematurely escaped parental boundaries and whose life now lies in broken pieces, there is still hope. The wise, sensitive parent must lead that child to the only place where lives can be put back together again. It was for the sick and the sinner that Jesus Christ died. There is no life so enmeshed that He cannot untangle it. When sins are confessed to Him, He not only forgives, He removes them.

Life can begin again!

Postscript . . .

Let Me Be A Parent

Let me love my child.

Let me teach him right from wrong, as I understand
right from wrong.

Let me teach my child to love God, his fellowman
and his country.

Let me provide for my child a world free from worries,
decisions and responsibilities of adults.

Let me protect my child from all who would exploit
him.

Let me teach my child to respect authority in our
home that he may respect it through every area
of life.

Let me teach him the value of discipline in work, in
money matters, and in study.

Let me guide my child through the seven teenage years
without undue interference from outsiders.

Let me choose for him until he is old enough to choose
wisely for himself.

BROKEN BOUNDARIES/BROKEN LIVES

Let me say "no" to my child so long as I am
responsible for him.

Let me discourage my child from dreaming of rights
without responsibility.

Let me help my child assume responsibility
for his actions.

As I have given him life, let me guide his life,
and if need be, let me help him pick up
the pieces of that life.

He is my child.

He is my responsibility.

Let me be his parent.